NANCY REAGAN:
THE WOMAN BEHIND THE MAN

(A VOLUME IN THE PRESIDENTIAL WIVES SERIES)

OTHER BOOKS IN THE PRESIDENTIAL WIVES SERIES

SERIES EDITOR: ROBERT P. WATSON

Dolley Madison
Paul M. Zall
2001. ISBN 1-56072-930-9.

A "Bully" First Lady: Edith Kermit Roosevelt
Tom Lansford
2001. ISBN 1-59033-086-2.

Sarah Childress Polk, First Lady of Tennessee and Washington
Barbara Bennett Peterson
2002. ISBN 1-59033-145-1.

Frances Clara Folsom Cleveland
Stephen F. Robar
2002. ISBN 1-59033-245-8.

Lucretia
John Shaw
2002. ISBN 1-59033-349-7.

Jackie Kennedy: Images and Reality
Mohammed Badrul Alam
2003. ISBN 1-59033-366-7.

Betty Ford: A Symbol of Strength
Jeffrey S. Ashley
2003. ISBN 1-59033-407-8.

NANCY REAGAN:
THE WOMAN BEHIND THE MAN

PIERRE-MARIE LOIZEAU

Nova History Publications
New York

Coordinating Editor: Tatiana Shohov
Senior Editors: Susan Boriotti and Donna Dennis
Office Manager: Annette Hellinger
Graphics: Wanda Serrano and Matt Dallow
Editorial Production: Alexandra Columbus, Maya Columbus, Alexis Klestov,
        Vladimir Klestov, Matthew Kozlowski and Lorna Loperfido
Circulation: Ave Maria Gonzalez, Vera Popovic, Luis Aviles, Sean Corkery,
        Raymond Davis, Melissa Diaz, Meagan Flaherty, Magdalena Nuñez,
        Marlene Nuñez, Jeannie Pappas and Frankie Punger
Communications and Acquisitions: Serge P. Shohov
Marketing: Cathy DeGregory

Library of Congress Cataloging-in-Publication Data

Loizeau, Pierre-Marie.
  Nancy Reagan: the woman behind the man / Pierre-Marie Loizeau.
     p. cm. – (Presidential wives series)
Includes bibliography and index.
  ISBN 1-59033-759-X.
  1. Reagan, Nancy, 1923- 2. Presidents' spouses—United States—Biography.
I. Title. II. Series.

E878.R43L65 2003
973.927'092—dc21   2003011882

Copyright © 2004 by Nova History Publications, a division of
      Nova Science Publishers, Inc.
      400 Oser Ave, Suite 1600
      Hauppauge, New York 11788-3619
      Tele.: 631-231-7269   Fax: 631-231-8175
      e-mail: Novascience@earthlink.net
      Web Site: http://www.novapublishers.com

Printed in the United States of America

To Maryse, Emilie and Chloé

CONTENTS

ACKNOWLEDGMENTS

This book would not have been possible without the generosity and precious advice of Stewart Ross, a man of multiple talents. His keen observations and meticulous proofreading have been of invaluable help. Elizabeth Rushton, either on her regular office chair or in her temporary wheelchair, has also brought her share of proofreading and I thank her wholeheartedly for her assistance and encouragements.

I am very fortunate in having such friends as William and Catherine Clark, of Thousand Oaks, California. They made my research at the Ronald Reagan library in Simi Valley a very comfortable experience. I had the privilege of staying at their home all the while and being treated as a spoilt child. I cannot forget Kirk and Connie Redmond who are at the very origin of this project.

I also want to thank the archivists at the Reagan Library for their professionalism and constant availability. Shelly Jacobs, in particular, facilitated my access to research materials.

Finally I owe a special debt to my favorite trio – Maryse, Emilie and Chloé who have served as a sympathetic audience. Thank you for their patience, support, and love.

Thank you all very much.

FOREWORD

Robert P. Watson

The old saying that "behind every successful man is a woman" is perhaps nowhere more evident than in the White House. Even a cursory examination of the wives of presidents reveals a group of remarkable individuals who made many contributions to the lives and careers of their husbands, the presidency, and even the nation. Over the course of U.S. history first ladies have presided over state dinners, overseen extensive historical renovations of the Executive Mansion, held press conferences, campaigned for their husbands, testified before Congress, championed important social causes, and addressed the United Nations.

As a candidate for the presidency speaking of the role his wife would assume in his administration Bill Clinton stated that when the public elects a president, they are getting "two for the price of one!" To an extent such a statement has always been true. First ladies have been a viable part of the presidency since the nation's founding. Of the men who served as president during the country's history, nearly all of them served with a first lady at their side. Only a handful of presidents have held the office without their spouses. For instance, both Andrew Jackson and Chester A. Arthur had lost their wives prior to their presidencies; Rachel Jackson dying in the interim between her husband's election and his inauguration and Ellen Arthur just prior to her husband's Vice Presidency. The wives of both Thomas Jefferson and Martin Van Buren passed away years before their presidencies. But they were exceptions. Only two bachelor presidents have been elected, Grover Cleveland and James Buchanan, however the former married while in office. Three presidential wives died while serving in the White House: Letitia Tyler, Caroline Harrison, and Ellen Wilson. However, both President John Tyler and President Woodrow Wilson later remarried while in office.

Presidential wives have served without pay and, until very recently, often without proper recognition. So too have they wielded political power and social influence despite the fact that they are neither elected nor appointed. In part because they are not elected or accountable to the citizenry and in part because of strict social conventions that precluded women from participating in politics for much of the nation's history, presidential wives have been forced to exercise their power and influence in a behind-the-scenes manner. Yet, in this capacity many wives have functioned as their husband's trusted confidante and private political advisor.

Presidential wives have faced great challenges, not the least of which include the loss of privacy and specter of assassination looming for themselves and their families. The presidency is arguably the most demanding job in the country and the challenges of the office are experienced by the president's family. Amazingly, several first ladies served while trying to raise a family. Presidential wives have faced severe scrutiny, an invasive press corps and curious public, and criticism from journalists and the president's political enemies. This is perhaps one of the experiences that all first ladies have shared. Not even popular wives like Martha Washington, Abigail Adams, or Jacqueline Kennedy were spared from harsh personal attacks.

The first ladyship has been the "unknown institution" of the White House. For most of its history it has been ignored by scholars and overlooked by those studying national and presidential politics. However, this is slowly changing. The public, press, and scholars are beginning to take note of the centrality of the first lady to the presidency. A new view of the president's spouse as a "partner" in the presidency is replacing more traditional views of presidential wives. Even though the Founding Fathers of the country gave no thought to the president's wife and the Constitution is silent concerning her duties, today the "office" has become a powerful, recognized institution within the presidency, complete with staff and budgetary resources that rival the so-called "key" presidential advisors.

It is also an intriguing office whose occupants are no less fascinating themselves. Indeed, the presidential wives are a diverse lot that includes new brides barely out of their teens to grandmothers who had spent a lifetime married to men that would become president. There have been women of refinement and wealth and there have been wives who would seem ill-prepared for the challenges of the White House. And of course, there have been successes and there have been failures.

The first ladyship is one of the nation's most challenging and dynamic public offices. So too is it an office still in development. In the words of First Lady Barbara Bush, concluding her remarks when delivering the commencement speech at Wellesley College, "And who knows? Somewhere out in this audience may even be someone who will one day follow in my footsteps, and preside over the White House as the President's spouse. I wish *him* well!"

In the volumes of this Series the reader will find the stories of women who fashioned the course of American history. It is the goal of the publishers and myself that this book and each volume in the Presidential Wives Series shed light on this important office and reveal the lives of the women behind the American presidency.

I hope you enjoy this book and the entire Series!

Robert P. Watson, Series Editor

PREFACE

The public perception of the First Lady has evolved through the years and the press and scholars are beginning to take note of the essential role presidents' wives have played in the Administration and in the nation as a whole. Their participation in the country's historical, philosophical and sociological experience has made them "First Women" and "First Partners". They have been identified as standard bearers of the whole female community, as they have both pioneered and reflected women's role in American society.

The twentieth century in particular has seen the construction of their image in the media and highlighted the evolution of their political role at the heart of presidential power.

Although she had never taken much interest in politics, Nancy Reagan was thrilled when her husband Ronald left his acting career to enter the world of politics and run for Governor of California in 1966. She became his partner ever since.

As a former actor, Ronald performed well before the cameras and the public and because of this positive image, maintained a high degree of popularity during most of his political career. He was known as "the Teflon president" for criticism seemed never to take hold of him. Nancy's Hollywood career had been shorter but she also knew how to make the most of her knowledge of studios and show herself to best advantage. Yet for a few months, she was one of the lowest rated First Ladies in American history. Amazingly, she then topped the list of America's most admired women.

Today, in many polls about First Ladies, Nancy Reagan still ranks among the last.

She has often been criticized as "the power behind the throne", wielding influence behind the scenes.

"You were always political partners. Weren't you? He depended upon you," CBS reporter Mike Wallace once asked Nancy on *60 Minutes II*.

"Well, that could be," she answered. "but I wasn't a politician."

Her answer seems to highlight the ambiguous role she played for almost three decades, from her years as First Lady of California to the time when she left the White House. Was her position as the political partner she admitted to have been so different from that of a true politician? In other words, wasn't her political power more real than she said and wrote?

To some extent, elements from her childhood provide an explanation to her attitude in the White House : her father's abandon, her mother's absence, her rapport with her stepfather, etc. These partly explain her feeling so insecure, her clashes with the press, her recurrent tensions with her children, her conspicuous consumption, her conspicuous love for her husband, her "adoring gaze" at him, her fears for his safety, her belief in astrology, her role in the firing of several Cabinet and staff members, etc.

Has Nancy Reagan been underrated, misunderstood, unfairly criticized? Have her qualities (clear-sightedness, rigor, moral rectitude, empathy, her positive image abroad, etc.) been too often ignored? To what extent has she expanded or limited the undefined institution of the First Lady?

The book seeks to explore the ambiguity that underlies this First Lady's multiple facets. It intends to shed light on the particularities of one of the most controversial yet exceptional women of the twentieth century and get a deeper insight into the complex role of the (first) lady they called "the woman behind the man".

PHOTOS

Engagement photograph of Ronald Reagan and Nancy Davis, January, 1952

The Reagans with Bill and Ardis Holden right after the Reagan's Wedding at the Holden's house in Toluca Lake, California. 3/4/52

Ronald Reagan and Nancy Reagan at the
"Stork Club" in New York City in the early 1950s.

Newlyweds Ronald Reagan and Nancy Reagan cutting their
wedding cake at the Holden's house in Toluca Lake, California. 3/4/52.

Ronald Reagan, son Ron, Mrs. Reagan and daughter Patti
outside their Pacific Palisades home in California. 1960.

Ronald Reagan and Nancy Reagan aboard a boat in California, August, 1964.

Ronald Reagan, son Ron, Mrs. Reagan and daughter Patti. 1967.

1981 Inaugural Family Photo: (standing from left to right)
Geoffrey Davis, Dennis Revell, Michael Reagan, Cameron Reagan,
President Reagan, Neil Reagan, Dr. Richard Davis, Ron Reagan
(sitting from left to right) Anne Davis, Maureen Reagan, Colleen Reagan,
Mrs. Reagan, Bess Reagan, Patricia Davis, Patti Davis, Doria Reagan. 1/20/81.

President and Mrs. Reagan pose in the Blue Room for their official portrait. 3/4/81.

President and Mrs. Reagan standing in front of their
Ranch house at Rancho Del Cielo. 8/13/81.

Mrs. Reagan surprises President Reagan with a birthday cake
during a White House Press Briefing. 2/4/83

Nancy Reagan riding a tandem bicycle with son Ron Reagan
on the south grounds of the White House. 4/22/81.

Mrs. Reagan laying flowers at the Omaha Beach
Memorial Cemetery, Normandy, France. 6/6/82

President and Mrs. Reagan await the arrival of Premier Zhao Ziyang of China at the White House Diplomatic Entrance. 1/10/84.

1985 Inaugural Family Photo: (from left to right) Bess Reagan, Maureen Reagan, Dennis Revell, Neil Reagan, Michael Reagan, Ashley Marie Reagan, Colleen Reagan, President Reagan, Cameron Reagan, Patti Davis, Mrs. Reagan, Ron Reagan, Doria Reagan, Geoffrey Davis, Anne Davis, Dr. Richard Davis, Patricia Davis. 1/21/85.

Official Portrait of The Reagans. 6/3/85.

President Reagan presents Mother Teresa with the
Medal of Freedom at a White House Ceremony. 6/20/85.

Mrs. Reagan at a "Just Say No" rally at the White House. 5/22/86.

President Reagan giving speech on the Centennial of the
Statue of Liberty, Governor's Island, New York. 7/4/86.

President Reagan with Mrs. Reagan inside
George Washington Hospital four days after the shooting. 4/3/81.

President Reagan and Mrs. Reagan pose on their
35th wedding anniversary at the White House. 3/3/87.

Official portrait of President Reagan, Nancy Reagan, Vice President Bush and
Barbara Bush on the White House colonnade. 8/11/88.

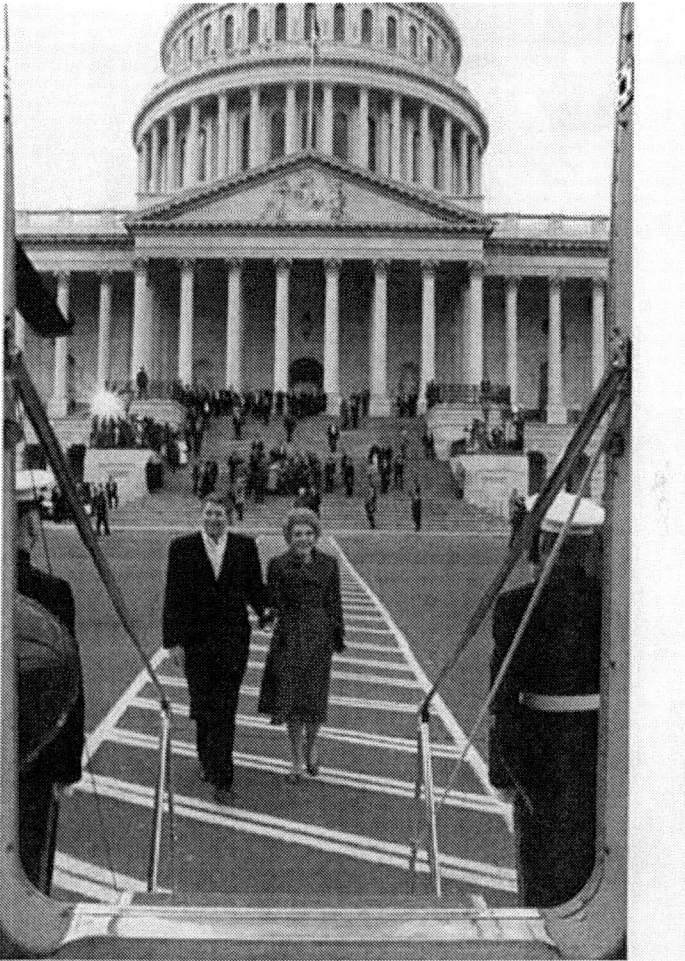

Last Day of Administration, The Reagans boarding the
Helicopter to the leave the U.S. Capitol, Washington, DC. 1/20/89.

Part I

FROM LONELY ANNE FRANCES
TO PROUD NANCY DAVIS

First version: According to Mrs. Reagan, Anne Frances Robbins was born on July 6, 1923. She gave her first cry in a New York City hospital whose name she does not remember, and no records remain because it burned down "years ago".

Second version: Anne Frances Robbins was born in Sloane Hospital, Manhattan. The building never burnt down. Her birth certificate carries the date July 6, 1921. When she grew up, Mrs. Reagan took two years off Anne Robbins' age to produce a younger identity.

So who is telling the truth, Mrs. Reagan or Kitty Kelley, the author of *Nancy Reagan: The Unauthorized Biography*? Does it really matter? Probably not. Still, how peculiar that such basic facts of modern history, concerning such a well-known person, have never been clearly and officially established!

"Nancy" was the nickname that Anne's mother, Edith Luckett, gave her. Edith, whom her friends called Dee Dee, was an itinerant dramatic actress. Nancy's father, Kenneth Seymour Robbins, was a very attractive young man whose irresistible charm Edith had easily and hastily succumbed to. He seemed to have all the qualities a young woman could dream of. He was good-looking, fun-loving, considerate, with a fine word for all circumstances. What is more, he belonged to a wealthy old New England family which had made a fortune and acquired great respectability in Massachusetts. His great-grandfather, Deacon Luke Francis, was one of the founders of Pittsfield, Massachusetts. His grandfather, Captain Frederick Augustus Francis, was well known as a Civil War hero. His father, John N. Robbins, was vice-president of W. E. Tillotson Manufacturing Company, a woolen mill at Silver Lake, Massachusetts. Kenneth himself had received an excellent education, attending a military prep school and Princeton.

What a difference from Edith's own modest background! She came from Petersburg, Virginia, where she was born on July 16, 1888. Her father, Charles Edward Luckett, used to work in Washington, D.C., for the Adams Express Company, later renamed Railway Express. The meager salary he brought in was hardly sufficient to support his wife, Sarah Frances Whitlock, and their nine children. Edith never really suffered as a child since she was surrounded by love and affection but times were hard, and all she had known during those years was sacrifice and frugality. Not quite.

Thanks to her uncle, Joe Whitlock, her mother's brother, who was a theater manager in Richmond, she was able to escape the poverty of her family and be initiated into the pleasures of acting. She got her first role on stage as a stand in for a child actor who had fallen ill. The character she played was to die and she did it so well and convincingly that the audience was in tears. To avoid the confusion between fiction and reality, the child raised herself up and waved at everybody to "reassure" them. This combination of talent and innocence that the child displayed with amazing spontaneity won over the hearts of the audience and produced such emotion that she received a long ovation.

From that moment on, she never really left the theater and school became history. She pursued her way as a full-time actress and managed to get a few parts in Broadway where she met some great performers of the day, such as David Belasco and George M. Cohan. She made friends with Alla Nazimova, a famous Russian actress who had started working on stage as a student of Stanislavsky in Moscow and who had then emigrated to the States. Edith got one of her first major roles in 'Ception Shoals, a play in which Nazimova starred. Among her celebrated acquaintances were also Walter Huston, Zasu Pitts, Colleen Moore, Louis Calhern and Spencer Tracy all of whom later became movie stars. Someone had nicknamed her "Lucky", which she was indeed.

At the age of nineteen, Edith suspended / interrupted her career and married the well-heeled, well-bred twenty-three year old Kenneth. But for the new Mrs. Robbins, life did not take the turn that was expected. The honeymoon was short-lived and the fairy tale she had dreamt of as a little girl did not come true. Kenneth revealed a personality that Edith, blinded by love, had not noticed before. After two years at the war, sweet and charming Ken decided to have a carefree comfortable way of living and made no effort to make his wife happy. Devoid of ambition, he chose to earn a living as a car salesman in New Jersey rather than join the family business. He continued to have fun and behave as "a rich playboy who's not worth the powder to blow him up," refusing to accept his status as a married man[1]. Not even as a father. He was not present when his child, Nancy, was born.

Edith was deeply hurt by his absence.

She called her baby "Anne" in honor of an ancestor of the Robbins family, Anne Ayres, who was known as the first Episcopal nun in America and for helping found St Luke's Hospital in New York City. She chose "Frances" for her middle name, which was also her own mother's middle name. The prospect of bringing up a child alone worried her enormously. But she was strong and resilient enough to overcome the difficulties. Nazimova agreed to be the baby's godmother. As a modern woman, Edith, whom her friends had by now definitively nicknamed "Dee Dee", decided to take on her responsibilities as a mother while continuing her acting career. She carried Anne Frances from theater to theater and for two years, while her mother was performing on stage, the little baby girl remained backstage in a trunk that served as a cradle. She was the company's sweetest attraction; she was part of the scenery, so to speak, and they all adopted "Nancy", as her mother had nicknamed her, as their favorite fellow traveler.

But traveling like gypsies, from town to town, from one theater and hotel to another, was not a life of a two-year old, Dee Dee thought. She wanted her daughter to be brought up in "normal" conditions. The baby needed a stable environment, a permanent home where she could sleep peacefully and lead a quiet life. It was in Bethesda, Maryland, at her elder sister's home, that Dee Dee found such a place. "Aunt Virginia" and "Uncle Audley" had bought a little Dutch colonial house in Battery Park, a new suburban residential area. They agreed to take care of Nancy while her mother was on the road. They had a daughter too, Charlotte, who was three years older. The two cousins got along very well. Charlotte, at five, was soon adopted by Nancy as her big sister, the one that she could play games with, that she followed all the time and trusted as both her protector and adviser. Whatever Charlotte said was gospel, wherever she went was the place to go. Nancy loved playing hopscotch, "Kick the Can" or "Statues" with her cousin. Charlotte did not seem to have faults. She was not even afraid of cats and dogs. She had a wire-haired terrier, Ginger, which they once decorated with red, white and blue ribbons for a Fourth-of-July parade. Aunt Virginia was a very good person too. She was the queen of the kitchen and prepared the most delicious cakes a little girl could dream of and enjoy for real, which partly accounted for Nancy's chubby cheeks and puppy fat. As for Uncle Audley, he

---

[1] The words of Mrs. Richard Rowland to Colleen Moore. In Laurence Leamer, *Make-Believe: The Story of Nancy & Ronald Reagan* (New York: Harper and Row, 1983), p. 21.

always had a candy treat for the kids when he came home from work in the evening. Nancy liked those Saturday nights when he would take them to the cellar, pick up a family-sized bar of milk chocolate and give them a large piece. It was not much but as Nancy recalled later, "When you don't have a lot, small treats loom large."[2] She also enjoyed playing catch with Charlotte and her father during his free time. He was always very affectionate with her and when she felt sad or cried, he would give her big hugs, make her laugh, carry her in his strong arms, tell and read her stories, almost like a real father. He *was* the father Nancy did not have.

Living with the Galbraiths was really pleasant and Nancy never missed anything, except one precious thing: her mother's presence. Yes, she felt terribly lonely without her mommy. That feeling was particularly acute during the "bad days", as when she argued with her cousin or neighbor, or when she was ill. Once, as she was lying on her bed with double pneumonia, she wanted her mother so much that she cried with anger: "If I had a child and she got sick, I'd be with her." To soothe away Nancy's feeling of being abandoned, Aunt Virginia would take her to New York by train whenever Dee Dee arrived there for a performance, so she could spend time with her mother. They would stay in a hotel or apartment for a few days or weeks depending on Dee Dee's schedule. Words cannot express the exhilarating experience of those delightful moments. How wonderful it was just to be with "mommy"! Nothing could feel better than the natural effusion of motherly love and affection. They spoke and played a lot together. Nancy loved the sound of her mother's voice, warm and sweet and reassuring. Nothing wrong could happen with mommy's presence and the whole world seemed to be brighter and safer. With Dee Dee, Nancy gradually got a sense of what acting involved: the makeup, the costumes, the prompting, and backstage effervescence during a performance. She liked watching her mother's shows from the wings, which she considered a privilege, but most of the time she sat in the audience and was thus initiated to both sides of theater life. But she was not old enough always to differentiate acting from the real world. During one performance, as her mother played the role of a woman dying, Nancy started to cry as she thought her mother had passed away for real. She wailed so loudly that Dee Dee had to rise from the dead and wave to her daughter to comfort her and for the performance to continue. "It's not real. It's make-believe. It's a play and I'm playing a part," Dee Dee explained to her backstage.[3] The tears did not last too long and Nancy enjoyed her mother's job, although this was not a notion she could fully

---

[2] Nancy Reagan, with Bill Libby, *Nancy* (New York: Berkeley Books, 1980), p. 13.
[3] *Make-Believe*, op. cit., p. 25.

understand. With her little child's eyes, she was fascinated by the scenery, the rise and the fall of the curtain, the intermissions, the laughter and applause of the audience – the whole glamorous theater atmosphere. Of course she was too young to grasp all the difficulties that lay behind the job like the bad days, the poor roles and the irregular wages … Nancy wanted to be an actress, just like mommy.

Nancy really loved those visits, but like all good things, they were always too short and there were too few of them. When time came to separate after a few days together, it was a real wrench to leave in opposite directions, for both mother and daughter. Fortunately, once in a while, Dee Dee would find the time between performances to come to Battery Park. Those visits were delicious moments for Nancy. Her mommy was seen as the glamorous star from Broadway and everyone admired her. Nancy was fascinated, almost hypnotized as she sat watching her performing in the center of the small living room, acting out a few parts from her latest play. Dee Dee always had gifts for the children. Once she brought her daughter a wig with long blond curls like Mary Pickford's. Nancy wore it everywhere with great pride. Instinctively she visualized herself on the stage like her mother, or in the movies, and she too would become a star, like her mother. She loved dressing up with Dee Dee's stage clothes, using her make-up, and acting like the real actress she wanted to become.

The fall of 1926 saw Nancy's first experience with the school system. Aunt Virginia and Uncle Audley wanted the best for her, as for their own daughter, so they decided to send her to one of the top-ranked private schools in Washington: Sidwell Friends School. It was rather expensive but they made a point of paying for her education themselves, at least for the first two years. Then Dee Dee saved enough money to take over.

Going to school was a tiring four mile trolley ride down Wisconsin Avenue from the Galbraiths' home. But the presence of Cousin Charlotte helped little Nancy forget about the daily effort. At Sidwell, Nancy became aware of the privileges that went along with wealth. Indeed she and Charlotte rubbed shoulders with richer children some of whom were chauffeur-driven to school in big limousines. They were the children of White House officials, Washington city councilors, leading businessmen or prominent lawyers, who owned much bigger houses than the Galbraiths', somewhere in the very elegant nearby community of Edgemoor.

Nancy occasionally went to Verona, New Jersey, on the Robbins' family estate, to see her father, but time had separated them forever and she could not think of him as her real father. The distance that separated them was not only material. It was characterized by an emotional vacuum, an absence of affection that turned to indifference. Ken had remarried and was a stranger in her life.

Curiously, Nancy felt more comfortable speaking with his wife. But it was his father's mother, Anne Robbins, "Nanee", that she liked most. She was a handsome, gray-haired woman who sprayed herself with violet toilet water. She was always good and caring towards Nancy, her only grandchild of whom she was the only grandparent. They liked to talk together and take walks around the estate.

Nancy's life took a new turn in the year 1929. One beautiful early spring day, Dee Dee came to visit her in Battery Park and told her that on a recent sailing trip to Europe, she had met a man with whom she had fallen in love. Loyal Davis was the "doctor she wanted to marry," only if she agreed of course.[4] If she did, Dee Dee would give up the stage and they would all live together in Chicago. Nancy was somewhat perturbed by the idea of marriage and having to share her mother's affection with a stranger. But her hesitation was soon wiped out by the prospect of having a real family life, the absence of which she had so suffered from. Dee Dee left Nancy again for a short period, as she had to go back to Chicago with Walter Huston and finish her *Elmer the Great* tour. A few weeks later, Aunt Virginia and Nancy headed off together by train to Chicago. The heat wave that struck the Mid West that year made the trip long and tiring. It seemed to be in keeping with Nancy's own psychological unease at the thought of leaving a place that she was used simply to calling "home", abandoning the Galbraiths with whom she had shared so many wonderful moments and more than anything else, losing her cousin Charlotte, her best friend, her "sister". As Nancy recalled later, "Those were good old times in the good old days, a peaceful time in a peaceful place". The separation from those familiar surroundings, even the tiny little space on the upstairs porch that had been converted into her bedroom, was a hard test to endure for a six (maybe eight?) year old. Still, she would be with mommy at last. As they arrived at the train station in Chicago, they were met by Dee Dee and her fiancé, Dr. Loyal Davis.

On May 21, Nancy served as a flower girl at their wedding in a small chapel at the Fourth Presbyterian Church on Chicago's North Michigan Avenue. Both bride and groom were starting a second marriage. For Nancy, it was also a second life that was beginning. She lived in a huge elegant apartment on East Delaware Place for a while and later moved to Lake Shore Drive in another commodious richly furnished apartment overlooking Lake Michigan and with a spectacular view.

Dr. Loyal, as she called her new stepfather, was an eminent neurosurgeon, professor and chairman of the Department of Surgery at Northwestern and

---

[4] *Nancy*, op. cit., p. 15.

Passavant General in Chicago. Life with him was not an immediate success as Nancy had to adjust to someone she did not know and, to tell the truth, she was a little bit overawed by the stern-looking man. But she gradually developed affection and respect for him, which grew steadily into deep attachment. As she recalled later in her autobiography *Nancy*, he was "a man of more strength and integrity than any I have known other than Ronnie, and as I grew up I came to understand this and to love and respect him."[5] The doctor had a little son, Richard, from his first marriage who was a couple of years younger than Nancy. He lived with his mother, Pearl, in Beverly Hills until she died in 1939, at which time he joined his father and became the fourth member of the family.

Loyal Davis had been born on January 17, 1896 in Galesburg, Illinois, the only son of a railroad engineer. Dissuaded by his father from doing the same grueling job, he decided to pursue medicine. Through hard work and perseverance, though he came from a modest family, he attended Knox College and Northwestern University where he encountered the elite world of neurosurgery. He served his residency at Cook County Hospital and was trained by Boston's Harvey Cushing, considered as the father of American neurosurgery. He first worked as an associate at Peter Bent Brigham Hospital in Boston and then returned to Chicago as the first full-time brain surgery specialist in the town. He became one of the leaders of American neurosurgery, was a founder of the American Board of Surgery and American Board of Neurological Surgery, served as chairman of the board and president of the American College of Surgeons. As a researcher, he edited several journals such as *Christopher's Textbook of Surgery* and *Surgery, Gynecology and Obstetrics* and also wrote several books intended for specialists of his medical discipline. He was a man of many accomplishments and medical or paramedical innovations. He created a helmet that protected American pilots from shrapnel wounds during the Second World War. He elaborated a very effective remedy to treat high-altitude frostbite injuries. He was selected to participate in a surgical mission in Moscow in 1944. His undisputed talent and high medical performances were rewarded in 1945 as he was legitimately honored with the Legion of Merit medal.

Dr. Davis had a real passion for his job and crusaded against the shady business and inadequacies that had pervaded the medical profession. He publicly denounced the unfair practice of fee splitting whereby physicians referred their patients to specialists and surgeons from whom they received a share of the fees. He spoke out against the dangerous growing habit of granting medical licenses to unqualified doctors who could perform surgery without the necessary training and

---

[5] *Ibid.*, p.16.

competence. He led an unrelenting campaign against doctors whose fees yo-yoed according to their patients' insurance. He also fought vigorously to favor surgery only as a last resort solution and prevent unnecessary mutilations. His battles often triggered a rash of counterattacks and caustic criticisms. But he was a man of principles, who remained independent and faithful to these principles. He was known at Northwestern as rigorous, uncompromising and a strict disciplinarian. In the list of instructions he gave to the new students, the first one was to wear a suit and tie, like any respectable doctor in America. He said that clothes and attitude determined your personality. He seemed to have a compulsive aversion to litter and filth. He could not stand the sight of cigarette butts his interns sometimes negligently threw on the floor, or of a toilet that was not flushed. To avoid the latter inconvenience, he rigged up a system so that whenever a stall door opened or closed, toilets flushed automatically. Generations of medical students and interns feared Dr. Loyal for his severity, and many were angry with him but did not dare rebel openly. It does not mean they remained inactive. When they went into poor black neighborhoods to deliver babies, they slyly persuaded mothers to name them "Loyal". It was their own way of showing their strong aversion to the doctor's racist and bigoted attitude and contempt of the poor. When the doctor got wind of the practice in the black ghettoes, he flew into such a fury that he put a notice on the bulletin board ordering interns to stop their pernicious influence in the naming of black children.

Dr. Loyal was no less scrupulous and meticulous at home than he was at work and did not tolerate any scrap of paper on the floor, a closet door left open or a dirty dish lying around in the kitchen. Everything had to be neat, clean and orderly. He was a "rock-hard disciplinarian" and a non-stop perfectionist. Nancy was too young to realize that even adults feared the man she herself was living with now. For her, he never appeared as a man to be afraid of. He always demonstrated that he loved her as if she were his real daughter. And she wanted to be loved by him. For that, she learnt to be very clean and very neat and a perfectionist herself. That way, she knew she could earn his approval and merit his love. Upon her request, he once gave Nancy his own definition of happiness: "Nancy, the answer to happiness is almost twenty-five hundred years old and it's basically what the Greeks said. It's the pursuit of excellence in all aspects of one's life," a precept that Nancy tried to comply with ever after.[6] She wrote:

He added a dimension to my life I am sure I would not have had without him.... Some people you meet in your life make you stretch to reach your fullest

---

[6] Chris Wallace, *First Lady: A Portrait of Nancy Reagan* (New York: St. Martin's Press, 1986), p. 7.

capabilities. I found my new father to be one of these people.... He always demanded the best of you and made you want to give the best you had.[7]

Neatness and an obsession with perfection certainly belonged to that new "dimension" acquired by Nancy. It would remain as a distinctive mark in her character and would follow her ever after, through her college years, through her Hollywood years, as a wife, as a mother, as a First Lady.

Yet, it was not always easy for Nancy to satisfy the man without hurting the capricious nature of the child she still was. As they were once walking past a candy store in a Chicago street, Nancy was suddenly and "irresistibly" attracted by a chocolate candy displayed prominently in the middle of the store window.

"Daddy, would you buy that for me?" she asked immediately with an ingratiating smile.

"No, dear, that is too rich," he replied as a good father caring about his daughter's health.

"But, Daddy, I *want* it!" she insisted, seeking immediate satisfaction. She started to cry and cry louder to test her father's patience and get him to yield under pressure.

"But, Nancy, I told you that I will not buy that candy for you." Dr. Loyal rejoined, imperturbably.

She cried again, on and on, stamping her feet, kicking and screaming like a baby, insisting desperately for her father to give in. Nothing happened. Of course it was hard for a little girl to understand the reason for his refusal but he did explain why excessive consumption of candies could damage her health, cause acne, or cause diabetes. And it was also a good opportunity for Nancy to realize that children could not get everything they asked for and that restrictions were part of life, whatever your age. Naturally Nancy was allowed to eat candies and chocolate bars like all children, but with a doctor at home, consumption was under control. Dr. Loyal never acted arbitrarily and whenever required, he explained clearly and concisely the validity of his decisions. Punishment, which was not the only educational method he used, was always justified. He was "strict but fair". Responsibility and excellence were his master words.

He acted the same with his interns. They would curse him behind his back, alternately denouncing his lack of humor, his constant moralizing and self-righteousness or his dictatorial teaching methods. They accused him of being aloof and dour, pompous and despotic. But these immediate judgments often lacked the necessary maturation of time and experience, for with hindsight, the

---

[7] *Nancy*, op. cit., p. 16.

same people modified their appreciations and recognized the wisdom of his actions and their initial resentment and exasperation little by little turned into respect and admiration. He was indeed an excellent teacher who wanted to draw the best from his students. He assumed that only hard work and self-discipline could make indisputable professionals. And though he might have appeared too severe at times, he never failed to put his extensive knowledge and experience at the service of those he instructed. "They knew where he stood but more importantly, they knew *why*."[8]

In announcing the union of Edith Luckett and Loyal Davis in its society section the day following the wedding, the *Chicago Tribune* described the happy couple as having the same age: "Both Dr. Davis and his bride gave their ages as 33 years."[9] In fact, Edith was 41, that is eight years older than her husband but looking much younger. One of the questions that most friends and relatives of the Loyal household posed in the early years was how such a stern surgeon could get along with a happy-go-lucky actress. Opposites attract, goes the saying. She was uninhibited, talkative, outgoing, laughed and joked a lot, liked to dance and have fun. He was quite reserved, over-delicate and straitlaced. Yet he enjoyed having a happy, cheerful wife, sparkling with gaiety and vitality. She was what he could not be but would have liked to be. For Edith, he represented the stability, the security and the status she had sought for all these years. When they had guests, she would have some music on after dinner and be the party leader. She would invite her quiet husband to dance around the room and spur the rest of the party to join them. She would tell jokes, even vulgar ones, but they sounded acceptable in the joyful atmosphere she created. Even Dr. Loyal would laugh. Edith was the center of attraction, the star. One significant anecdote of the Davis clan was reported by Richard ("Dick"), Nancy's stepbrother. One night, during a Christmas holiday, as the family were gathered at the dinner table, Nancy expressed her worries about having to memorize sonnets by Keats and Shelley for her English literature class at College. Dr. Loyal decided that the four of them would learn parts of the poems to help her. The initiative pleased Nancy enormously but "this pursuit of excellence" was first and foremost Dr. Loyal's delight. Or was it? Suddenly Nancy's mother, Dee Dee, got up from the table and naturally displayed her talents as an actress, dancing around the room and parodying the sonnets with a little improvised rhyme of her own about "Mr. Sheets and Mr. Kelly." As Richard recalled, "this was the light-hearted side of our home life, and it was a

---

[8] Roger Elwood, *Nancy Reagan: A Special Kind of Love* (New York: Pocket Books, 1976), p. 43.
[9] Kitty Kelley, *Nancy Reagan: The Unauthorized Biography* (New York: Pocket Star Books, 1991), p. 19.

good counterbalance between a very serious and intent father and a mother who had a really wonderful sense of humor."[10]

Dee Dee's voice was soft and clear, and her power of elocution had been well exercised during her acting years so that she could alternately declaim classical poems and play the most hilarious buffoon. Her oratorical gift even attracted the attention of the mayor of Chicago, Edward J. Kelly, who asked her to help him with public speaking. Kelly, a Democrat, had been appointed at City Hall in 1933 after the incumbent mayor Anton Cermak had been killed. Dee Dee's help must have been effective because he stayed in power for fourteen years, until 1947.

Dr. Loyal, a hard-line ultra-conservative, was fiercely anti-Roosevelt, anti New Deal. His Republican friends included Barry Goldwater, the senator from Arizona who would be the presidential nominee in 1964 against L. B. Johnson. Yet despite the radical differences in their political convictions, there was mutual respect between Edith and Dr. Loyal and they were very protective of each other. She helped him with his GOP fundraising operations and he did not mind his wife's tutoring the Democratic mayor. He was even proud to see his wife move in the élite circle of the top politicians in town.

In fact, Edith, known to everyone as "Edie", was so genial and lively that she drew people to her like a magnet. She was a woman of many good causes, working indefatigably as a volunteer, throwing herself into charitable work, dedicating herself to fundraisers for the Fourth Presbyterian Church. She enjoyed doing hospital rounds with her husband, comforting his patients, fraternizing with his students. She decided to start a gift shop at the hospital and endeared herself to most people, whether doctors, nurses, patients or even visitors. Edith also worked professionally as she was hired by NBC Radio to act in soap operas, a job for which she made good money. She played Bob's mother, the funny Mrs. Drake, or Gardenia, the black maid in "The Betty and Bob Show". In the summer, when Charlotte came on vacation for a few days, Nancy and her cousin would go to the NBC studios and watch Edie perform. She continued broadcasting for other soaps such as "Ma Perkins", "Broadway Cinderella", or "Stepmother" until 1944.[11] Edith had so many friends from the Broadway and Hollywood world: Walter Huston, Colleen Moore, ZaSu Pitts, Myron Selznick, Reginald Denny, Louis Calhern, Spencer Tracy etc. The Davises enjoyed giving teas, luncheons and cocktail parties, mixing his colleagues in the medical professions with her friends from the show-biz. The result was a sophisticated combination of celebrities, the cream of the Chicago social scene to which Mr. and Mrs. Davis now belonged.

---

[10] Wallace, op. cit.
[11] Kelley, op. cit., p. 21.

The stern-looking neurosurgeon was not by nature a man of this world, it was forced on him by his wife's inclinations. But he certainly took advantage of the situation as it helped him establish credentials in the Republican arena.

Nancy continued visiting her birth father in New Jersey a few times, though she felt alienated from him. They were almost like strangers to each other. Once, things turned badly. He made an improper remark about Edith so that Nancy, who loved her mother so much, felt deeply hurt and defended her. She flew into such a rage she said she wanted to leave. He got angry too and locked her in the bathroom for punishment. Though Robbins apologized when he realized his mistake, it was too late. The damage was done and it was the last visit. Nancy would never forgive the man and would never forget the incident. She confessed years later that it was one of the most traumatic events she went through in her childhood and since then she developed a feeling of claustrophobia each time she was in a confined place. "I dislike locked doors and feel trapped behind them", she wrote. Ken Robbins had no place in her heart any more. Her real father was now Loyal Davis.

Nancy so much wanted to please the doctor that she sometimes went on trips with him to visit patients. She accompanied him at Northwestern, watching him work in his office or laboratory. Some week-ends, he would take her into the operation room where he performed brain surgery. Though the experience was a rare privilege that only a surgeon's daughter could enjoy, it was definitely not her favorite activity but she knew he would be proud of her. It was the price to pay to deserve his love.

She did feel herself as his daughter but there was still an inner frustration that hindered the full recognition of their mutual affection. Whether she liked it or not, her name was still Nancy Robbins, and she found it hard, if not humiliating, to bear. All her friends had the names of their fathers, which seemed so obvious. Why not her? He was her father affectionately, emotionally, but it was definitely not good enough for her happiness to be complete. In secret, she craved to be adopted by him. One evening, little Nancy took her courage in both hands and knocked on the door of a neighbor, Orville Taylor, whom she knew was a retired attorney. The visit of the young lady somewhat surprised the old man. She looked so serious.

"Judge," she said timidly, "I've come to see you on business."

"What is it, Nancy?" he asked, in a reassuring tone.

"I'd like to know how to adopt Dr. Davis," she explained.

"That's a little difficult", answered the judge, scratching his head with embarrassment, "but I think it can be arranged."[12]

As soon as Nancy had left, the jurist called Dr. Davis to tell him about the visit. The doctor was moved by the little girl's courageous initiative. "I've always wanted that", he said, his voice broken with emotion. "But I didn't know how to approach Nancy or her mother."

There was a law that permitted adoption if it was the child's choice. The only restrictive clause was for the child to be fourteen. Months went by and when Nancy reached the required age, she brought the subject up again. Dr. Loyal assured her that more than anything else in the world he wanted her to be a Davis. The only condition left was for her to meet her biological father and get his consent with the assurance that he would not oppose the adoption in court. During a vacation, she gathered the legal documents for her father to sign and all alone she headed off to New York where she met him at the Waldorf-Astoria. Ken Robbins still loved his daughter sincerely and was awfully sorry for all the mistakes he had made in the past and was bitterly disappointed at the idea of losing her. But his remorse did not curb Nancy's determination to get his signature. She could not be moved by him anymore. At her insistence, with a broken heart, he eventually signed, finding some small comfort in the feeling of making his daughter happy. Nancy knew her grandmother, "Nanee", whom she had developed tender affection for, would be terribly affected too, if not shocked, but the decision had been made and there was no going back. No regret. She returned with the precious papers to Chicago and presented them to the lawyer. Her petition, which was filed in the Cook County Circuit Court, was agreed to and she became officially "Nancy Davis". "You can call me Nancy Davis from now on," she loudly and proudly proclaimed to her classmates."[13]

Nancy's new status reinforced her already well established bonds with Dr. Loyal. By obtaining the adoption of the powerful and caring doctor, thereby officially formalizing her attachment and devotion to him, she demonstrated one significant trait of her character, one that she would retain all her life: her ability to "choose, acquire, and keep the man she loved." Observers thought that as she grew older, she was even more like Dr. Loyal than her mother, so she seemed like his natural daughter. She developed a meticulous, disciplined and perfectionist character like the surgeon's. Nancy admitted that Dr. Davis shaped her thinking and views on life. Though she was never really interested in politics before

---

[12] Leamer, op. cit., p. 31.
[13] Kelley, op. cit., p. 28.

adulthood, her new father's conservative political opinions certainly greatly influenced the way she entered the political world years later.

The 1930s saw the Great Depression close in tightly upon America, a hitherto prosperous country unprepared for an economic crisis of that scale. It started under the Republican Hoover administration with the Stock Market crash and the subsequent bank panics. Poverty struck the major regions, hitting big urban centers as much as it did remote country villages. Shanty towns, known as "Hoovervilles", were built by homeless sufferers. Farmers went bankrupt. For many, the depression was simply a "gut issue": eating or starving. Franklin Roosevelt launched his New Deal program to lessen privations and soften the harshness of the economic situation. At home, Dr. Davis was firmly opposed to state intervention and raged against the Democratic president. The Depression did not seem to affect Nancy very much. Poverty was the least of her preoccupations as she was sent to Chicago's exclusive Girls' Latin School which only privileged children could attend. She stayed there from 1929 to 1939.

The institution observed a draconian discipline, which was rather in keeping with Nancy's constant search for perfectionism. The dress code was exemplary: uniforms for everyone. Jewelry, lipstick or makeup of any kind were strictly forbidden. Sloppy desks were not tolerated. The school had a favorable reputation in academic milieus for preparing students to college in the best conditions. The classical curriculum it taught, with its balanced amount of academic subjects and sports had produced generations of solid, well-trained and talented students.

Nancy was an average student in her class but she was definitely a hard worker. Her major problem was science with which she had serious difficulties and for which she admitted total incomprehension. But all in all, her grades averaged B minus, which, given the high standard of the institution, was quite honorable. She excelled at talking and writing about contemporary events. The years were marked by Hitler's irresistible rise to power. His expansionist policy precipitated Europe into the state of war. In September 1938, a pact was signed in Munich with European heads of state Daladier, Chamberlain, Mussolini and Hitler granting Germany the right to occupy the Sudetenland. The Gestapo arrested 17,000 Jews and deported them to a no man's land between Germany and Poland. Synagogues were burnt, Jewish stores plundered and Jewish citizens arrested, stigmatized with yellow stars, and interned in concentration camps. Nazi Germany's consecutive annexations of Austria, Bohemia and Moravia and the invasion of Poland inevitably led to the war. Though it was very attentive to the evolution of events and remained on its guard, the United States was not directly involved in the conflict. Its population was not yet fully aware of or did not feel really concerned by what was happening overseas. Some, like Loyal Davis, were uncompromising isolationists, advocating non-intervention in European affairs. Nancy was not very keen on politics but her interest in diplomatic matters and world issues earned her good grades in such subjects as history, geography and writing. But what she liked more than anything else were the movies and the world of stars. She already knew some of Hollywood's celebrities through her mother's acquaintances, like Spencer Tracy. Her favorite actor, though, was Tyrone Power. All the girls of the time were more or less secretly in love with Tyrone Power! His gorgeous athletic physique, even more than his undeniable talent as an actor, nourished a good many schoolgirl conversations.

Nancy enjoyed the many opportunities the school offered for activities. She was president of her sophomore class, of the Dramatic Club, sang in the glee club, played field hockey, basketball … But though she was a serious and assiduous student, she also spent much energy in dances and parties. Her school was just a few blocks from Boys' Latin School which her brother Dick attended. There were joint activities, and social life was quite active. Every other week, she and her classmates attended a dance organized by the Fortnightly Club. She liked the boys there. She and her friends enjoyed watching the boys' football and basketball games. As she later confessed, "I always had a crush on someone."[14] There was Bobby Crane of the R.T. Crane plumbing family or Buddy Baird of Baird and Warner Real Estate, but they were not real love matches. A student from Boys' Latin, Sangston Hettler, Jr., *was* her first serious "crush". Tall and red-headed, he looked like a typical Irishman. He came from a rich family which had made a fortune in lumber. Nancy and "Sock" –that was his nickname– went out together as much as they could. He offered her his signet ring and their idyll was known by everyone in the two schools. Once, they were mentioned in the gossip column of the *Chicago Herald-American* and a photograph of the couple even appeared in the newspaper, leaving no doubt about their future engagement. She did continue to date Sock for quite a while until she met another suitable party with whom she soon fell equally deeply in love. Life was fun for Nancy and boyfriends were not her only concern. She also enjoyed working for good causes and helping the "less fortunate" as Dee Dee and Dr. Davis would say. Once a week, she entertained children at the Martha Washington School for Crippled Children, worked with the Service Club Follies or raised funds to buy guide dogs for the Seeing Eye Dog program. In the summer, she would go to Lake Geneva with her family. She would swim and sail on the lake, play tennis, golf and even go to dances there.

During her senior year, she became a leader and after being defeated for the student body presidency, she was elected as student judge, a role she took most

---

[14] *Nancy*, op. cit., p. 41.

seriously. She was responsible for enforcing the school's rules and was merciless with offenders. But the best role she played in high school was elsewhere. She was president of the Dramatic Club and, as everyone admitted, the best actress in the school. The high point of her high school years certainly came when she had the lead in the senior play, *First Lady*, a 1935 comedy by George S. Kaufman and Katharine Dayton. Nancy, who played the prophetic title role of first lady, was the undisputed leader in the group. She knew everyone's part by heart. During the rehearsals, she advised and directed the other members of the cast, and on the opening night, she prompted or improvised to cover for those who had forgotten their lines. The play, which was very popular in those days, and was adapted to the screen in 1937, portrays the fight two women lead against each other to put their husbands into the White House. She played one of the two rival heroines aspiring to the title of "First Lady" and who, through treason and maneuvering, achieves her goal. On stage, the once shy Nancy disappeared totally to merge into every little cell of her character. Her rigor and sensitivity made her the real first lady of Girls' Latin theater. But without treason. For the Chicago press, as well as for all the spectators, she was simply "cute little Nancy".

Nancy's adolescent years were rich in events, discoveries and passions. Like her mother, she was nicknamed Lucky, and rightly so. Vacationing with friends, going to summer camp, traveling to Bermuda, she was a privileged girl in many ways. But not spoiled. At her coming out, beautiful and radiant with joy among the other debutantes, she appeared more mature, self-confident, well prepared for her entrance into society and ready for new adventures in life.

As she recalled much later: "Those were wonderfully happy days."[15] The 1939 Girls' Latin yearbook probably gave the most authentic portrait of Nancy at the time and captured her character and personality most accurately: "Nancy's social perfection is a constant source of amazement. She is invariably becomingly and suitably dressed. She can talk, and even better listen intelligently, to anyone from her little kindergarten partner of the Halloween party, to the grandmother of one of her friends."[16]

After graduation from high school, she went to Smith College in Northampton, Massachusetts. The place is one of the Seven Sisters, the female equivalent of the Ivy League and is known as the world's largest resident liberal arts college in the world. It is a "socially correct" school, attended by upper middle class women, daughters of businessmen, bankers, doctors, lawyers... Nancy and her high school friend Jean Wescott ("Whitey") had longed to go there

---

[15] *Ibid.*
[16] Leamer, op.cit., p. 39.

but when they arrived, they found the other beginners a bit sophisticated with their accents from Boston or New York. The school was one of the most prestigious in the country, including 2,500 students and a high reputation faculty of 250. Dr Davis and Edith selected it for Nancy as being the right place to meet the right people and get the right education. Despite the prestige, the students were not all hard workers and there were a lot of parties and dances. Nancy was no better at science there than she was at Girls' Latin. She majored in English and drama. She did particularly well in the latter discipline. She acted in several college plays and was fairly popular. During the vacations, she acquired real experience in theater as she was recruited as an apprentice in the local New England summer stock theaters and playhouses. There she did all jobs, from running errands through working at the ticket office to painting scenery, upholstering furniture or cleaning out the actors' dressing rooms. She did also appear on stage quite a few times.

A new man arrived in Nancy's life during that period. Nancy organized an afternoon tea dance at the Casino Club in Chicago for her debut –a tradition which in those days marked the formal beginning of adult life. Her mother had been careful enough to arrange the big day –December 28, 1939– so she could invite the boys of the Princeton Triangle Club who were presenting their annual show in Chicago, along with the standard Chicago crowd. The "coming out" was to start at 5 o'clock in the evening, and Dr. Loyal had made Nancy nervous with his insistence on punctuality. Her nervousness increased as few guests were on time. Would the others come? One of the early arrivals was a man from the Princeton Triangle, Frank Birney. Seeing that Nancy was worried, he set out to ease the tension by amusing her. He made a real show by pretending to be various people, having different names and using different accents, coming in and out and going up and down the receiving line again and again, as if everyone had arrived. He was truly funny and had Nancy and the guests present bursting out laughing. He charmed everybody and filled most pleasantly the time spent waiting for the latecomers. Suddenly everything was fine and smooth. No one was missing and the party was a great success. Nancy was all radiance and glitter in her virginal white *mousseline de soie* gown with its silver lace bodice, holding her nosegay of white carnations and white narcissus. Edie also looked beautiful and youthful in her blue silk dress. Dr Davis conversed with the best and brightest of his élite guests. The band played waltzes, young and less young couples danced frenziedly and everyone enjoyed themselves.

During that period of her life, Nancy went to a string of other coming-out parties, Elizabeth Stenson's, Barbara Bennett's, Helen Dick's, Grace Shumway's, Barbara White's, Virginia Skinner's, Betty Gillespie's, Priscilla Blackett's, Whitey's… There was also New Year's Eve to celebrate. Late December 1939 was nonstop partying and dancing. It was certainly not the real world young adults were to expect for their whole life but it was definitely a milestone in Nancy's existence, and a beautiful one indeed.

Nancy started dating her coming out party rescuer, Frank Birney. They had a lot in common: he was from Chicago, had attended a prestigious school –Lake Forest Academy–; his parents were divorced, and like Nancy, he loved dancing. He liked writing skits, which for the theater loving Nancy, was not an insignificant detail. She might be acting in one of his plays one day. She found him funny, witty, delightful. She was in love again. Despite the long distance between Northampton and Princeton, they saw each other on a regular and serious basis –that is as often as possible. Nancy would go down to Princeton for football games or dances, Frank would drive up to Smith for dances. Or they would meet "under the clock" in the lobby at the Biltmore Hotel in New York City for a romantic week end. There had been other rich college boys with whom Nancy had had "crushes", but none had been as serious as the experience she was going through now. Marriage prospects were in the air after eighteen months together.

At Smith, Nancy belonged to a group of student actors called "Bander-log". The name was borrowed from Rudyard Kipling's monkey people whose life was preserved thanks to their mimicking. The college Bander-log started putting on a musical comedy with short skits that were full of college humor, satirizing their own student life-style and mimicking the films and cultural creations of the time. The show was entitled *Ladies on the Loose*. The male roles were played by students from Amherst. The group rented the local high school auditorium for the two evenings of the show, for a modest $50. They would charge students and parents and give the profits to charity. The opening night took place on December 5, 1941. As the curtain rose, a chorus of twenty traveling girls sitting on their suitcases sang:

> We're not very subtle and never abstruse,
> Frankly, we're ladies just on the loose,
> Beware of the smoothies of domicile fame,
> We're Dianas out for game!

They were hilariously funny. Nancy, who had a leading part, appeared in the second musical number wearing a hat of bananas and spoofing Carmen Miranda, the then popular Latin actress:

> I've read books about south of the border,
> I've learned every rhumba by heart,
> I took Madame Lazonga's six lessons,

I'm a good neighbor right from the start.
The word "manana"
Rolls off my lips
When they shake their maracas
I shake my hips.

Nancy received a standing ovation. She was showered with praise for her sweet, sensuous voice and her natural acting talent. The other numbers were just as well received and after the two evenings, Nancy had become a star.

The next morning, radios blared out the tragic news. The Japanese had bombed Pearl Harbor, one of the American military bases in Hawaii. At Talbot House, where the troup had come down to breakfast, all the fun of the previous night instantly disappeared. The performance was forgotten. No more maracas and shaking of hips. The reality revealed how fragile and ephemeral happiness was. The initial shock was followed by an uneasy feeling of incomprehension and fear. One of the girls, whose boyfriend was a Marine Reserve, began to cry. Life was taking another turn.

For Nancy, the roaring winds of the war were echoed by another more personal blow. Frank Birney was going to meet his half-sister in New York. As he was late and had rushed to catch his train, he had jumped the gate at Princeton Junction and had taken a shortcut by running across the railroad tracks. The driver of an oncoming train saw the young man but could not slow his train down. Frank was killed instantly.

The police investigation did not clarify the mystery of his death. Had it really been an accident? Could it have been suicide? Frank had been depressed recently. He had been worried about his grades and in danger of flunking out of Princeton, he had been worried about the war and the world situation. He had been worried about Nancy. They were not seeing each other as often and he could not stand the idea of her playing in a college musical with Amherst boys. Was it the ultimate act of a man desperately in love? One of Frank's close friends declared some time later: "I went to his room after we identified his clothes and I found the suicide note addressed to his mother and father in his wastebasket. I took it and said nothing to any of the other guys, but I gave it to Frank's brother-in-law. Then we concocted a story for Frank's mother – he had been extraordinary close to her – that he had been accidentally hit by a locomotive going seventy miles an hour engulfed in fog."[17]

Nancy never confirmed or denied the motives of Frank's death. Forty years later, in her autobiography, she gave her own version of the tragic circumstances.

"We were to meet in New York one weekend. I was waiting for him when the telephone call came. (…)"[18] Was her distortion of the facts a confession of the guilt she felt? Or just her own way of soothing the pain that was still hurting her after all these years? She wrote: "While now I wonder whether I had really been in love with Frank or whether we would ever have married, it took me a long time to get over his death. I felt a deep loss then and a little scar still remains inside, but I learned that life goes on and you go on with it." After the funeral, Nancy spent much time with Frank's mother. They were both in deep mourning and the slight comfort of each other's company alleviated their grief. It was a long time before Nancy could date other boys.

Life on the campus was different when she came back in January 1942. The whole nation was enduring the restrictions of the war and Smith was no exception. A new consciousness had swept over the college residential houses. Most students participated in the war effort. They were all "Rosie the riveter" in their own way. Some girls knitted sweaters for the Red Cross, others learned how to pack parachutes. There were special courses on first aid, radio communications, or flying. Some helped nearby farmers harvest their crops. The daily chores of dish washing or bed making were now assumed by the students themselves. The gas shortage entailed man shortage as well as the visits to Amherst were limited.

In her senior year, Nancy's interest in theater was reactivated by Hallie Flanagan Davis, the new drama teacher who had come from Vassar to head Smith's first Department of Theater. The woman's temper was as hot as her red hair but she was respected as a great professional and was well-known in the national theater circles.. The former head of the Federal Theater program, she impressed the students with her sharp eyes, strong voice and alert mind. Most of all, her charisma was an incredible boost. Nancy won a part in *Susan and God* but her major role came with *Make with the Maximum: A Factory Follies*, a song-and-dance review, written and staged by students and meant to entertain war workers. They played at Smith but also at the Fiske Tire Plant in Chicopee and several other factories throughout New England. Nancy played the role of the rich "glamour girl" who complained about wartime deprivations:

I miss my Nassau winters and Paris in the spring
My butler's making nuts and bolts
They've rationed everything
And it's simply impossible to find an extra man
The town car is in car storage

---

[17] Kelley, op. cit., p. 43.
[18] *Nancy*, op. cit., p. 43.

The yacht is in disrepair
And when I start complaining –
"Sorry, madame, c'est la guerre."[19]

Nancy started to date again, and her new beau was Jim White, a senior at Amherst. He seemed the perfect match again: handsome, impeccably neat, well-groomed, and he loved drama too. He and Nancy were deeply in love. After being stationed in Chicago in the navy for three months, Jim was transferred to the South Pacific. With the separation, Nancy took her life into her own hands, determined to throw herself into the war effort. Identifying herself with Dr. Loyal who had enlisted and was now Lieutenant Colonel in the Army Medical Corps, she set out to take a nurse's aide course and volunteered at Passavant Memorial hospital, where she used to watch Dr. Loyal perform surgery. She also took a job as a salesclerk in the college shop at Marshall Field's, one of the largest department stores in Chicago. Once she saw a woman steal a piece of jewelry and chased her to the elevator insisting on an immediate return of the goods. The shoplifter snatched at her button-down dress and ripped it open down the front. Fortunately, the security soon came to her rescue and apprehended the woman. Nancy was reprimanded for stopping the woman within the store limits, but yet she was rewarded for her toughness with a twenty-five dollar check and felt very proud. Working at the hospital also had its share of occasional dramas. As she was giving a patient a bath, she was worried about his lack of cooperation and absence of answer to any of her questions. He made absolutely no effort to help her. She asked a doctor to come in and see what was wrong with the man. The diagnosis was quite clear: the man she had been bathing was dead!

When Jim was on leave, Nancy visited him in California and they decided to get engaged. Dee Dee and Dr. Loyal, who was back from his army assignment, arranged an engagement party in their apartment. Jim's parents came all the way from Winchester, Massachusetts and brought Nancy a gorgeous Tiffany diamond ring on behalf of their son, who was back in the Pacific. The society columns of the *Chicago Tribune* announced the couple's engagement, but Nancy had made sure the wedding would take place "after the war", a decision which was not uncommon at the time.

Being in love with a military man seemed to be a patriotic act, as if it were a contribution to the war effort. "It was a heady, exhilarating time, and I was swept up in the glamour of the war, wartime engagements, and waiting for the boys who were away."[20] But within a few months, Nancy realized she had made a mistake

---

[19] Leamer, op.cit., p. 53.
[20] *Nancy*, op. cit., p. 44.

and was not ready for marriage. Though it was not an easy thing to do after the party and the paper announcement, she broke off the engagement and returned the ring. Jim would not be her husband, but they remained good friends ever after.

After she graduated from Smith in the spring of 1943, Nancy continued her job as a nurse's aide, but she felt insecure and vulnerable for a while. Where was her life going? She seemed to be prone to failure, losing her boyfriends and having no clear-cut career ahead. Yet she was still eager to become a real actress, on stage, in the movies, dreaming of stardom. But was it not all teen age fantasy, college Utopia? Suddenly the real world appeared dull and dreary, tasteless and colorless.

And then the telephone rang …

Part II

THE HOLLYWOOD STARLET

Edith's long-time friend, ZaSu Pitts, called to offer Nancy a small part in the traveling company of a play called *Ramshackle Inn*. It was a comedy-melodrama about an old maid librarian who buys a rundown hotel near the ocean only to encounter ghosts, secret trunks while wandering through mysterious situations. The actress who had previously been playing the part was leaving and they needed someone urgently to substitute. Nancy did not hesitate a second. She had just a vague idea of what the plot was and did not know whether the play presented much artistic interest at all. But she did understand she was lucky and could not drop such an opportunity. The first role in a professional production is always the most difficult to get. Once you have been selected, then you have credibility. After that, when you contact or are contacted by agents or casting directors, you do not only have college plays and summer stock to present.

And though the role would be only three lines, it was *Broadway*! She soon joined the company in Detroit, where the play was trying out before heading to New York. She played the role of a girl being held captive in an upstairs room. "At one point," Nancy recalled, "I came downstairs, spoke my three lines, and was returned to my room. It wasn't much but it was a start, and I was out on my own with the best wishes of my parents."[1] The play opened at the Royale Theater on Broadway on January 5, 1944. ZaSu Pitts's presence in the cast had attracted a large audience but the play received poor reviews. Nancy was disappointed that her name did not even appear in any of them.

Disappointed but not disenchanted. She and her new friends continued playing New York's "subway circuit", in various theaters in Brooklyn, The

---

[1] Nancy Reagan, with Bill Libby, *Nancy* (New York: Berkeley Books, 1980), pp. 56-57.

Bronx, Long Island... Being ZaSu Pitts's partner was certainly an immense privilege and provided Nancy with great pride and excitement. It felt like being somewhat famous as well. Nancy had been bitten by the acting bug and a new page was now being turned in her life. She was determined to go ahead and pursue a career in acting.

She decided to stay in New York. For a while, she stayed at the elegant and fashionable Plaza Hotel, on Fifty-Ninth Street and Fifth Avenue, but she soon realized that, away from her parents, she was not rich enough to have a star's standard of living, and she moved to the more reasonably priced Barbizon Plaza. It happened that one of her Smith housemates also trying to break into showbiz lived there as well, so they decided to share a room.

New York City was itself a theater, a gigantic one swarming with eclectic people going to and fro along busy streets and avenues, in a nonstop cacophony of ambulance and fire truck sirens and taxicab horn honking. Hot dog vendors occupied every corner. Stores seemed bigger and in greater number than in Chicago. You could buy everything you needed and more in the Big Apple, do everything you wanted and more, at any moment of the day or night. Time seemed to take on another dimension, unlike any other place in the United States. But for young women fresh from college, away from their families and usual friends, living there was a challenge which only the strongest could take up. Because she felt lonely and unable to summon up the extra energy needed to adjust to the pulsating rhythm and hectic activity of the city, Nancy's friend eventually gave up and went back home.

Nancy was alone again and feeling insecure. Would she fail too? Had she not better return home like her friend? But then what would her parents say? What image would she project to them? She was proud enough to hate mediocrity and refuse to be a loser. Apprehension nurtured her determination to succeed. She decided to move into a fourth-floor walk-up apartment at 409 Fifty-first street. She sought other parts and worked as a hat model between various engagements to earn some money. Fortunately, her social life was reactivated as she dated boys who often invited her to dine out. She loved going to the Stork Club, a chic night-club where she rubbed elbows with the big shots of the New York media, such as Walter Winchell, the renowned gossip columnist. Never penniless nor starving, yet each time she went to that restaurant, she had her own peculiar way of saving a little bit of money. Making sure no one was watching, she would sneak one or two rolls of bread into her pocket for a morning-after breakfast. One night, Sherman Billingsley, the restaurant owner, sent over a little pack of butter with a note telling her that she would better appreciate her breakfast with some butter on his rolls.

She had chosen to stay on the Eastside because it was close to Uncle Walter Huston's apartment. Lilian Gish, the famous silent film star who was another of her mother's old friends, lived a few blocks away. They often took her out to dinner or to a show or special occasion. Spencer Tracy, another of her mother's friends, whom she had played with once, happened to live nearby too and Nancy used to go and watch him rehearse for *Rugged Path*. She found him a very talented actor. One day, "Spence" gave Nancy's phone number to Clark Gable, the number one movie star in the country, who was visiting the town. "The King" did call her and the young inexperienced actress had some dates with the legendary –and oh so attractive!– Clark Gable, making his numerous female supporters across the country extremely jealous! Incredible though it was, she was in his company at the theater, at restaurants, at baseball games and so forth. The fan magazines and gossip columns took the situation to their advantage and insinuated a growing romance between the most celebrated bachelor in the country and the young woman: "Has something at last happened to Clark Gable, something, to be exact, in the form of a slim, brown-eyed brown-haired beauty named Nancy Davis – that is changing the fitful pattern of his romantic life? Has he, in other words, finally found the Gable woman, for whom he is more than willing to give up the Gable women? The answer seems to be yes – even though, if it is a love at all, it is so far a love in hiding."[2] The truth is there was no romance at all. He simply enjoyed her sweet company as they visited the town, he could easily make her laugh and she felt important in his presence: "The secret of his charm", she explained, "was that he made whoever he was with feel important. He made me feel important, and I must say it gave my ego a boost."[3]

Spencer Tracy's son, John, a polio victim who was almost deaf and partially sighted, a handicap that resulted from childhood illness, came to town. For one week, Nancy showed him around art museums, Broadway shows, fine restaurants, elegant stores and she let him sleep on her living-room couch. He was a very pleasant young man and Nancy admired his courage. One night a girl who had dated him in California, so as to get to Spencer, was to take him out to dinner but stood him up at the last minute. He was very hurt by this ungracious cancellation but did not complain. The girl's indelicate behavior filled Nancy with indignation. She decided to call back and gave the sweetie a lesson in manners.

Nancy continued modeling for the Conover agency with much success. She could not hope to make an entire career with this job but at least it helped make both ends meet and even paid some extras.

---

[2] Laurence Leamer, *Make-Believe: The Story of Nancy & Ronald Reagan* (New York: Harper and Row, 1983), p. 58.
[3] *Nancy*, op. cit., p. 60.

She went on making the rounds of producers' offices and auditioning for plays. Auditions always presented the same humiliating but inescapable ritual of long queues of candidates and endless waits until her turn arrived and she read a few lines before the director and several assistants. As she would try to show her talent, she would feel their frowning eyes riveted on her and her only. She would do her best to hide her shyness, look self-assured and read her lines with confidence, but it was hard. She eventually managed to get a part in a play but her relief was short-lived. During a rehearsal, the director took her apart and, not without cynical faked embarrassment, said he was sorry but he thought she just was not right for that kind of role. She was fired and did not get a penny.

Her determination would eventually pay off. In 1946, she was engaged in a Broadway show, *Lute Song*, with Yul Brynner and the popular Mary Martin. It was a musical based on a fourteenth century Chinese tale. Nancy dyed her brown hair black and slanted her eyes like a real oriental girl. They first performed in New England for tryouts opening in New Haven and Boston before arriving triumphantly on Broadway at the Plymouth Theater on February 6, 1946. Nancy was excited because Dee Dee and Dr. Loyal were among the audience. This time, the show received great reviews and ran for six months.

She appeared in other plays including *Cordelia*, by George Batson, and the George Abbot production of *The Late Christopher Bean,* with ZaSu Pitts again. The latter was a touring show and she performed in front of her parents in Chicago. In most of her roles, she would portray the young ingénue, a character type that fitted her own natural personality. She was described as "a sweet and decorous girl" or "unusually attractive and talented."[4] Despite the glowing terms, she certainly was not revolutionizing Broadway or the theater scene in Chicago, still she was doing what she had always wanted to do and that was enough to make her happy.

We were entering the age of television, the new medium that was bringing entertainment into every home, in or out of town. Of course, its growing success widened the spectrum of career opportunities for actors. Nancy did work for television and landed a role in the TV production of her first stage play *Ramshackle Inn*, again with ZaSu Pitts and in another show called *Broken Dishes*. Benny Thau, vice president of Loew's and casting director for Metro-Goldwyn-Mayer, saw her play. The man had come to New York to meet Spencer Tracy, who had given him Nancy's phone number. She accepted a blind date and the two went to see a play starring Tracy. "Nancy, why don't you come out and make a

---

[4] *Ibid.*, p. 79.

screen test?" Thau asked, most persuasively.[5] Nancy called her mother, who called Spencer Tracy, who contacted George Cukor in Hollywood to have him handle the test. Howard Keel played opposite Nancy and one of the best cameramen, George Folsey, shot the scene, a sequence of the forthcoming movie *East Side, West Side*. The test was successful and Nancy was signed to the seven-year standard contract for starlets and a $250-a-week salary to start.

Nancy was asked to fill out her M.G.M. studio biographical form. She gave her birth date as July 6, 1923, which because of Hollywood standards of youth, meant that a deduction of two years would have been more faithful to reality.

What job would she take if she were not an actress? "Lord Knows!"

Her favorite actors? Spencer Tracy, Walter Huston, Laurette Taylor, and her godmother, Alla Nazimova.

Her childhood ambition was "to be an actress".

And what was her greatest ambition now? "Sure to have successful happy marriage." Despite her thrilling new life as a starlet, the ideal "husband and children" dream still occupied a great place in her mind.

Did she believe in hunches? "Yes."

Was her life governed by any rule or rules? "Yes. Do unto others as you would have them do unto you. I believe strongly in the law of retribution – you get what you give."

What were her phobias? "...superficiality, vulgarity, esp. in women, untidiness of mind and person – and cigars!"

Any superstitions? "All of them and then some."

This new turning-point in her life happened in the spring of 1949. She began making her first film, a B-picture, almost immediately. It was called *Shadow on the Wall*, starring Zachary Scott and Ann Sothern. She got another small role in *The Doctor and the Girl*, with Glenn Ford, Charles Coburn and Janet Leigh. But her first important appearance came with *East Side, West Side*, directed by Mervin LeRoy and whose script she knew from her screen test. She had to play a scene with Barbara Stanwyck, which made her a little nervous, but the result turned out to be quite satisfactory and she was congratulated by the star. On her side were also such great names as James Madison, Ava Gardner and Cyd Charisse.

Nancy was gradually establishing herself in the industry and she felt more and more confident about her future. In the fall of 1949, as she was shooting one of her biggest roles with *The Next Voice You Hear*, Nancy urged her producer Dore Schary and his wife Miriam to introduce her to Ronald Reagan. She had already

---

[5] Leamer, op. cit., p. 63.

seen some of his films and relished his good looks. He headed her list of
Hollywood's most eligible bachelors and she was eager to meet him. They
arranged a little dinner party for her and the handsome actor. "I knew what he
looked like and I liked that," she said later: tall, brown skinned and brown haired
cowboy hero type, hard as a rock, yet retaining an irresistible Mid-Western
charm.[6] They saw each other a few days later, again and again. The courtship
proceeded slowly but surely.

In her autobiography *Nancy*, Mrs Reagan brings a different account of her
first encounter with Ronald Reagan. It appears that the account in itself is
authentic but the events occurred a couple of years later. As she presents it, her
destiny was going to be changed forever by a funny episode in her life – funny but
initially very embarrassing for the young up and coming actress.

She had received communist propaganda in her mail, inviting her to
participate in party meetings. And this had happened repeatedly over the last few
years, starting in New York. Nancy, who was the antithesis of a communist
sympathizer, was upset and afraid for her career at a time when the famous
Committee on Un-American Activities was investigating alleged communist
influences in the movie industry. Lists of suspects had been made up and the
name "Nancy Davis" had appeared on one of them. Yet Nancy spoke to Mervin
LeRoy as she feared there might be a confusion that could be disastrous for her.
He arranged for an item to be written by Louella Parsons, a well-known *Examiner*
columnist, specifying that the "Nancy Davis" in question was a different person.

LeRoy took the matter very seriously and reassured Nancy. He told her he
knew the one person who could settle the problem for sure, the president of the
Screen Actors Guild. His name was Ronald Reagan. Reagan was a fierce anti-
communist who had testified as a friendly witness before the House Committee
on Un-American Activities and had worked as an informant for the FBI providing
names of actors whom he believed were communists. Nancy, who had already
seen some of his films, relished his good looks and had a rather favorable overall
opinion of the man. LeRoy called Reagan and told Nancy the man would call her
back. That evening, she kept waiting but the phone never rang. She saw Le Roy
the next day who told her that the Guild would defend her in case of a problem.
Reagan had mentioned that there were at least three other Nancy Davises in
Hollywood. But Nancy was not satisfied with that simple message, reassuring
though it sounded. She wanted to speak to Reagan herself.

"Nancy Davis? This is Ronald Reagan from the Screen Actors Guild. Mervyn
LeRoy asked me to look into your problem, and I have some answers for you. If

[6] http://www.pbs.org/wgbh/amex/reagan/filmmore/reference/interview/nancyreagan02.html

you're free for dinner tonight, perhaps we could talk about it then."[7] Mervyn LeRoy had convinced Reagan to call Nancy. She could not refuse such an invitation with such a handsome man. Two hours later, when she opened her door, she was face to face with a visitor leaning on two canes. The situation was quite unexpected for both of them. The athletic person she knew from movies looked somewhat different with canes but still he definitely was a gorgeous young man. Reagan had thought he might be greeted by another typical Hollywood starlet, snobbish, flashy, overexposing her good looks to seduce the man who could give her career a boost. Instead a young charming brunette, rather shy and demure, had been waiting for him and was introducing herself. She had a sweet smile and a soft melodious voice. He explained that he had broken his leg in a charity softball game and had spent two months in hospital. She felt sorry for him and guilty to have bothered him with her problem. In fact, he was not bothered in any way and off they went to LaRue's, one of the finest restaurants on Sunset Strip. He was a fine talker with a great sense of humor and she kept laughing as he told her his repertoire of anecdotes, one-liners, jokes and stories. What Nancy liked about Reagan, in addition to his looks, was that he was not self-centered like most other actors. His conversation was not limited to the glamorous Hollywood world. He loved history, in particular the Civil War. He had a passion for horses and talked about the small ranch that he owned in the San Fernando Valley. He also knew a lot about food and wine. When dinner was over, he suggested going to Ciro's where Sophie Tucker was opening that night.

"Fine," she said. "Just for the first show."

They stayed for the first show, and the second show. Time passed fast that night and it was past three in the morning when "Ronnie" drove Nancy home. She did not have much time to sleep but she slept in blissful peace. "I don't know if it was love at first sight", Nancy wrote later, "but it was something close to it. We were taken with one another and wanted to see more of each other. We had dinner the next night and the night after that and the night after that... We saw all the Sophie Tuckers I had missed in my life..."[8] The Nancy Davis's case of mistaken identity did not matter very much now. Yet Ronnie did present it to his associates at the Screen Actors Guild and had no difficulty convincing them of her innocence. She came from an irreproachable good conservative American family and should endure no further embarrassment. She was cleared.

Mrs. Reagan does not mention the dinner party at Dore Schary's in her autobiography and the Nancy Davis communist episode is wrongly timed. Still

---

[7] Nancy Reagan, with William Novak, *My Turn: the Memoirs of Nancy Reagan* (New York: Random House, 1989), p. 94.
[8] *Nancy*, op. cit., p. 102.

the fact remains that she and Ronnie got along well right from the beginning and soon became inseparable.

Ronald took her out to places of interest in Los Angeles where everyone seemed to know him and compliment him. There was always someone eager to exchange a few words with the president of the Guild. Nancy and Ronnie would talk for hours. Or more exactly *he* would, and she would be all ears. Her admiration seemed to have no limits. She was impressed by the quality of his speech, his powers of conviction and the perspicacity of his ideas. He could hold a conversation just about any imaginable subject, whether serious or light-hearted, matter-of-fact or emotional. Though he did not like talking about himself, soon his life held no secrets from her.

Ronald Wilson Reagan was born on February 6, 1911, to John "Jack" Edward Reagan and Nelle Wilson Reagan in a small apartment just over the Pitney General Store in Tampico, a small Illinois town. His father, who ran a shoe store, gave the yelling ten-pounder the nickname "Dutch" when he first saw him: " For such a little bit of a fat Dutchman, he makes a hell of a lot of noise, doesn't he?"[9] Jack was an Irish Catholic, his mother a protestant of Irish-Scottish descent. They both dearly loved Dutch and his older brother, Neil, two years older, whom they called "Moon". Jack's job as a shoe salesman did not bring a fortune, and times were hard. But the Reagans were a typical small town American family. They lived simply and happily. Yet their existence could have been happier had not Jack had a weakness for beer and whiskey. Once, on a cold snowy winter evening, Dutch came home and found his father sleeping, lying drunk on the front porch, after a day pub crawling. The boy dragged him into the house, upstairs, undressed him and put him to bed. That night, for the first time in his life, Ronnie felt deeply and sadly what the word "alcoholism" really meant. Jack's drinking problem gave him a poor reputation in the neighborhood and ruined his business several times. They moved five times in less than a decade eventually to settle in Dixon, Illinois. Despite the problems, Ronnie loved his father and he enjoyed going hunting and fishing with him and his brother. He was even proud of his father. What he was particularly proud of was his aversion to bigotry. Once, as Jack traveled for work, he checked into a hotel for a night. The clerk told him his sleep would not be perturbed by Jews as they were not allowed. Jack, who felt strongly about any form of discrimination, bluntly replied: "I'm a Catholic, and if you don't take Jews, I guess you don't want Catholics either." He walked out angrily and spent the night in his car. Another time, he forbade Ronnie and his brother to watch D. W. Griffith's *The Birth of a Nation*, because it glorified the Ku Klux Klan. Jack's

---

[9] http://www.americanpresident.org/KoTrain/Courses/RR/RR_Life_Before_The_Presidency.htm

life in Dixon changed for the better when, as a liberal Democrat and wholehearted supporter of President F. D. Roosevelt, he became director of the local Works Progress Administration, a federal program that aimed to stimulate the American economy during the Great Depression and provide unemployed people with useful work.

Dutch dearly loved his mother Nelle whom he resembled a great deal. She was a very pious person, a very affectionate mother and a natural do-gooder. She took the time to tell her children frankly about their father's alcoholism, explaining he suffered from a real illness, which was hard to cure, and more than anything else in the world, he needed their affection and their love to soften his pain. She was also an eternal optimist, a character trait that Ronnie got from her and for which he was thankful as he referred to it many a time in his adult life: "We were poor, but I never knew it," he often said.[10] Nelle was also a talented speaker and was regularly called upon to give readings at her Christian Church. Ronnie often praised her as the most dedicated and generous person, one who had a strong belief in human virtue. She would visit patients in hospitals, and bring Bibles and cookies to prisoners. Like her husband, she could not tolerate prejudice and would work for justice in her own way. She would defend blacks whom she thought had been unfairly arrested, fight for their release and take them into her home until they found a job.

Dutch went to North Dixon High School where, even though he was not a brilliant student, he received a serious and comprehensive education. He featured in many school plays for which he was rated an excellent performer, wrote for the yearbook and was elected president of the Drama Club and of the student body. He did a lot of sports, running track, playing basketball and making the varsity football team as a junior. He worked summers as a lifeguard at Lowell Park, a local recreational area, and made fifteen dollars a week. He also enjoyed the company of a "sparkling brunette", Margaret Cleaver, with whom he shared a passion for drama and much of his social life. After graduating, like Margaret, Dutch enrolled in nearby Eureka College in September 1928. He majored in astronomy and economics though he was not very "serious" with studies. But he revealed himself as an undisputed leader and like his mother, he became a remarkable speaker. As a freshman, he was chosen as student representative and he organized a strike to protest the decision of cutting out certain courses for budgetary reasons. The demonstration resulted in the return to the initial curriculum and the resignation of Bert Wilson, president of the college. He also worked as a reporter on the school newspaper, performed drama, was recruited as

---

[10] *My Turn*, op. cit., p. 107.

a lifeguard and swimming coach and became captain of the college team. To get some money, he washed dishes at his fraternity house, Tau Kappa Epsilon, and also in the girls' dormitory, confessing that the latter job was assuredly his favorite! After graduating, he began a career in broadcasting and landed a job as weekend sportscaster for WOC in Davenport, Iowa, making $10 per game plus transportation. 1932 was his first presidential election as a voter. His ballot was cast for Democratic candidate Franklin Roosevelt. After two years, he transferred to NBC's WHO radio station in Des Moines, where he was known as "Dutch" Reagan. Soon, he earned a comfortable $75 a week, which he used mostly to help his parents and send his brother through Eureka College. Then on a trip to California to cover the Chicago Cubs baseball team training, he was contacted by a Hollywood agent, Bill Meiklejohn. After a successful screen test, Warner Bros offered him a seven-year contract with a salary more than double what he earned at WHO. Dutch set out for California and began his motion picture career. *Love Is on the Air*, in which he coincidentally portrayed a radio announcer, was the first of the fifty films or so that he made in the next four years. He had leading roles but played in "B" films essentially, for which he was known as, and called himself, "the Errol Flynn of the B's". Then his career took a new turn as he was cast as George Gipp ("The Gipper") in *Knute Rockne—All American*, a film relating the life of the once popular Notre Dame football coach, in which Pat O'Brien had the title role. Reagan appeared in the famous deathbed scene where he tells Rockne to ask the team when things are tough "to win one for the Gipper". The role earned him the nickname "The Gipper". To most observers, his best performance came in *King's Row*, the highlight of his film career in which he played Drake McHugh, the character who in a poignant memorable scene cried out: "Where's the rest of me?" on discovering that his legs had been amputated. Thirty-four years later, when Reagan published his autobiography, he gave its title a dramatic tone by borrowing the famous line: *Where's the Rest of Me*.

It was during the shooting of his ninth film, *Brother Rat*, in 1938, that he met his first wife Jane Wyman, a former dancer who like him came from the Midwest. With her blond dyed hair and false eyelashes, she had taken on the typical 1930s' glamour girl image. One of her great pleasures was to sit at a table in night clubs with a big hat on her head while smoking a long cigarette in a cigarette holder. She had already been married to a New Orleans dress manufacturer, Myron Futterman, but their union had lasted barely more than a year. Ronnie, who had dated so many beautiful girls before, found Jane terribly attractive and soon told her of his feelings. They married on January 26, 1940 in Glendale and honeymooned in Palm Springs after the wedding. One year later, a baby girl, Maureen, was born on January 4. Four months later, unfortunately, he lost his father from a heart attack. Ronnie wanted another child, but Jane would not put her acting career at risk. They found a compromise by adopting a son, Michael, in 1943. Meanwhile, following the Japanese attack on Pearl Harbor, Reagan, a second lieutenant of cavalry in the Army Reserve, was called to active service. Nearsightedness kept him away from the front and for the next three years, rising to the rank of captain, he served at Ft. Mason in San Francisco, supervising the loading of convoys, selling war bonds, and narrating preflight training films for bomber pilots with the Army Air Force 1st Motion Picture Unit in Culver City. He also appeared in propaganda films for the army, such as *Desperate Journey* (1942), *Jap Zero* (1943) and *For God and Country* (1943). In 1943, he was cast in Irving Berlin's musical film *This Is the Army*.

While he was serving in the Army, Jane's movie career took off and her brilliant roles in *The Lost Weekend* (1945) or *The Yearling* (1946), for which she was nominated for an Academy Award, paved her way to stardom. Her efforts were rewarded in 1947 as she won an Oscar for her remarkable performance in *Johnny Belinda*, in which she played the role of a deaf mute girl impregnated by a rapist whom she eventually kills after he has tried to take the baby away from her. Unfortunately, the Reagans' professional and matrimonial affairs were not going the same direction. They developed a love-hate relationship that became hard to endure for both of them. What with the allegations of her affair with Lew Ayres, her co-star in *Johnny Belinda*, and her aversion to Ronald's non-stop talking. She once warned her friend June Allyson: "Don't ask Ronnie what time it is or he will tell you how a watch is made."[11] She simply had had enough of it, especially of political discourse. Sure he was a gifted talker but she was bored with his growing political interest. She would not endure any more of Republican maneuvers and Democratic tactics, of the Truman Doctrine and the Truman-Dewey election fight. Enough was enough. In 1948, she filed for divorce on grounds of "extreme mental cruelty." It became final on July 18 1949.

And now, in 1950, here he was, free as a bird, dating Nancy Davis. She was bringing him relief and peace, helping him assuage the pain he had suffered during the lengthy proceedings of his divorce. The scar was not healed yet but brighter days seemed to be looming ahead with the presence of a sweet creature like Nancy on his side. He had recovered his sense of humor and she was the ideal listener, absorbing every single word with a smile. Her wide eyes were turned on him in total admiration. They had one thing in common: both were very sentimental and believed in romance the old fashioned way. Yes, they were falling

---

[11] Frances Spatz Leighton, *The Search For the Real Nancy Reagan* (New York: Macmillan Publishing Company, 1987), p. 40.

in love. It had been harder for Ronnie to recognize it for his heart had suffered so much torment in recent months, but he was irresistibly drawn to her as she brought him comfort, support and affection. Admittedly he had dated a score of other girls after his divorce. They were actresses, like Virginia Mayo or Ruth Roman, models like Betty Underwood or singers such as Monica Lewis. They appeared as easily interchangeable preys for the attractive ladies' guy. In Ronnie's life though, these ladies served no other purpose than to take Jane out of his mind. He had long hoped that there was still a chance to save his marriage but reconciliation had proved just impossible. This transient period was a sort of catharsis, a necessary expiatory penitence and emotional purification process that would eventually release the weight of his conscience and refresh his state of mind.

Nancy stood out against this background of inconsistent adventures, shining bright where the others darkened. She had been determined to win his heart and clung tenaciously to her Romeo. No, he was not just another date, the relationship was serious and she felt mature enough to reveal her deep feelings. Like no one else before, she showed curiosity and interest in Ronnie's aspirations and ambitions, in his problems and inner feelings. Though he had put walls around him, she was the only one who could share the most intimate secrets of his personal life. She felt that love involved merging herself totally into her man's existence. Her determination to keep him just for herself, for ever, would overcome all obstacles. And obstinate she was. She understood that political action and his children's happiness guided his life and she promised herself to support him and help him reach his goals. She ran twice for Board membership of the Screen Actors Guild and was eventually admitted in 1951. As such, she remained a fervent supporter of her husband whose motions at the Guild she seconded for about ten years.

She soon met Ronnie's children Maureen and Michael, went to his new ranch near Lake Malibu and agreed to ride with the kids who appreciated her efforts with horses. She learned how to feed the animals and clean up and haul manure. She enjoyed helping out around the ranch like a real cowgirl. They would go hiking or play "wild games of tag in the pool."[12] She even learned how to cook scrambled eggs! She knew that this initiation into the simple life on a ranch brought her closer and irreversibly to the man she loved. Hollywood did not exercise as much attraction. Her priorities had shifted away from the superficial glamour and limelight into the essence of life.

---

[12] *Nancy*, op. cit., p. 113.

Ronnie and Nancy dated for more than two years before he eventually led her to the altar.

They were married on March 4, 1952, at the Little Brown Church in the Valley, outside Los Angeles. Their close friends Bill Arden and his wife Ardis served as best man and matron of honor. They were the only guests at a very private but memorable ceremony. They spent their first night at the famous Riverside Inn and the next morning, the happy couple headed for Phoenix, Ar., to honeymoon at the Arizona Biltmore where her parents used to spend their winters. Ronnie and Dr. Loyal instantly became friends and despite the difference in age, felt they had many points in common. They both believed in hard work and perseverance, having moved their way up from modest backgrounds to neurosurgery (Dr. Loyal) and acting (Ronnie). Though Ronnie was a Democrat, he was impressed by Dr. Loyal's conservative convictions. They had both been divorced but faithfulness was their idea of perfection and happiness. And the two men soon found out that they liked telling jokes and stories, vying for the funniest puns and one-liners –Edith was certainly the best in that field, though, but hers were bawdier than Dr. Loyal's— Nancy admired the two men in their own way. In her eyes, Ronald was the only man who measured up to Dr. Loyal.

Nancy was feeling lucky and happy. Her parents' lifetime love affair seemed to reverberate delightfully on her own marriage. She had everything she could possibly wish for in her existence. The feeling was pure elation.

"I've often said my life really began with Ronnie, and I think to a great extent it did. What I really wanted out of life was to be a wife to the man I loved and mother to our children. It seemed that everything else had just been a prelude to this."[13] More than once, Nancy was the target of mockery for a discourse that was perceived as anachronistic or affected, but her entire life seems to have confirmed the sincerity of her views on marriage and family and proved her detractors wrong. Her passion for her husband has survived the years. Boredom seems never to have set in.

For a few years following her marriage, Nancy continued acting, but less enthusiastically and less frequently. She appeared in *Donovan's Brain* (1953), a science-fiction thriller, *Rescue at Sea* (1955) a.k.a. *The Frogman* or *Crash Landing*, and in her last movie, *Hellcats of the Navy* (1957), a World War Two submarine novel adapted to the screen by director Nathan Juran, she co-starred with her husband. She played the role of Commander Casey Abbott's fiancée and confessed she enjoyed the love scenes. But she took her role with so much fervor that she had difficulty separating fiction from reality. As our heroine was to say

---

[13] *Ibid.*

goodbye to her sweetheart going off on a secret and dangerous war mission, she cried her heart out so convincingly that the shooting had to be stopped three times. "I began to cry—really cry", she remembered years later. "I guess there had been too many real-life good-byes in those days."[14] She certainly would not have sent her Ronnie off to war!

But after that experience, stimulating though it was, Nancy made the decision to stop acting. Now the whole film set excitement had disappeared and fiction had to give way to the real world. Definitively.

Nancy, now Mrs. Reagan, centered her life almost exclusively on her husband and, when they came, her children. Seven and a half months after she married, on October 22, 1952, she gave birth to a baby girl Patricia Ann, "Patty", by Caesarean section. Nancy took an immense pleasure in motherhood, much more than in cleaning and cooking. She had a housekeeper for that. "I know I said I wanted to be a wife and a mother; I never said I wanted to be a cook", she wrote emphatically in *Nancy*.[15] She devoted most of her days to Patti, doting on her, holding her tenderly in her arms, cuddling her, watching her sleep and babble, speaking to her with that unique language of caring mothers. And above all, the baby sealed her love for Ronnie. Her dream of perfection in life was coming true. They had moved into a cute little four-bedroom ranch on Amalfi Drive in the hills of Pacific Palisades, west of Los Angeles, close to the ocean, far enough from the Hollywood brouhaha. The house was special in Nancy's heart. Ronnie had planted an olive tree as a surprise gift when mother and child had arrived from the hospital after the birth.

Nancy was an affectionate mother, and surrogate mother as well when necessary. She got along pretty well with Maureen and Michael as they grew up. She saw through their presence a picture of her own childhood, still suffering when the memory of her heartrending days as an orphan would occasionally reemerge in her mind like an indelible trauma. Yet they were not her own children and having them around recurrently conjured up negative images of another woman in her husband's life. She always did her best to give them attention, tenderness and make them happy. "When I was a kid, I loved to have my back rubbed. I used to sit on her lap and would have her scratch my back," Michael mused years later.[16] But more or less consciously, she felt their presence prevented Ronnie's first marriage from being totally forgotten. In the same way,

---

[14] Nancy Reagan, *I Love You, Ronnie: The Letters of Ronald Reagan to Nancy Reagan* (New York: Random House, 2000), p. 69.

[15] *Nancy*, op. cit., p. 117.

[16] Chris Wallace, *First Lady: A Portrait of Nancy Reagan* (New York: Saint Martin's Press, 1986), p. 137.

Michael and Maureen realized they did not really belong to their father's new family. Maureen even called Nancy "the Dragon Lady"![17] Their frustration was enhanced by their natural mother's regular absence. Stardom kept her away from them as most of her time was devoted to work. They found themselves trapped in the middle of a Reagan Wyman-Reagan Davis blended family, unable to find their identity. They were sent to boarding school at a very early age and missed their parents enormously: "...at that time, it's a little tough to understand", Maureen later confessed, "because you think you're missing something and, of course, you are missing being at home."[18]

In late 1953, Taft Schreiber, an agent at MCA, found Ronald a job that brought the Reagan family the financial security Nancy had long aspired for. Ronnie became the host of the CBS weekly *General Electric Theater*, the popular Sunday night half hour television series, receiving a $125,000 to $150,000 yearly salary, not including a "fancy sum" from Revue Productions that Schreiber himself headed. Ronnie introduced each story and was to star in four programs per year, becoming more popular in the TV circuit than he had ever been in the world of movies. Very occasionally, Nancy made some brief appearances.

As the money flowed in, the Reagan family had a bigger house built, perched a little higher up in the exclusive Riviera area at 1669 San Onofre Drive in Pacific Palisades, hidden from outsiders' view, built around its swimming-pool and overlooking the Pacific Ocean. The spectacular view of nature at its best filled Nancy with great delight. She had worked with architect Bill Stephensen to make the sprawling residence her "dream house". She had wanted it perfectly to her taste, with everything to match: bright colors and soft pastels, lots of red, her favorite color, yellow couches, lots of antiques, etc. An exquisite combination of wood, stone and glass emphasized the indoor-outdoor spirit, a design Nancy was particularly keen on as if she had wanted to dismiss the painful memories of her childhood confinement. Outside, the stone gate opened on a paved driveway that was lined with thick hedges and trees. Beyond, the white azaleas, bright bougainvilleas and dense rhododendrons gave the place its colorful and "cheerful" tinge that perfectly reflected Nancy's (and Ronnie's) current upbeat feelings. To make their happiness a long-lasting one, Ronnie had symbolically drawn a heart with their initials in the cement of the patio and outside their bedroom.

Ronald Prescott, "Skipper", was born five and a half years after his sister Patti, on May 20, 1958, again by caesarean. Raising her two young children almost by herself, as Ronnie was busy with his job most of the time, was not easy

---

[17] Michael Reagan with Joe Hyams, *On the Outside Looking In* (New York: Zebra Books, 1988), p. 84.
[18] Wallace, op. cit., p. 138.

for the thirty-seven-year-old, yet inexperienced, mother. She wanted her children as "neat and orderly" as she and Dr. Loyal were, but she turned out to be too demanding and overprotective. As a reaction, both Patti and Ron would later become caught up in the turmoil of the 1960s' counterculture, which would considerably strain the parent-child relationships.

The children went to nursery school at John Thomas Dye, a private school in Bel Air. Ronnie and Nancy were both involved in the school, as much as their schedule allowed. She became a member of the Mothers' Club board and he helped out at the annual May Day school fair.

Gradually the Reagans were acquiring a rather exclusive way of life and belonged to rich America. They began mingling with the social crème of Southern California. It started through acquaintances at the kids' school where Nancy met and became friends with Mary Jane Wick, the mother of C. Z. Wick, one of Patti's little friends. Her husband, also named C. Z., had founded the Wick Financial Corporation and Mapleton Enterprises. Ronald and C. Z. soon struck a friendship too. Nancy and Mary joined an exclusive women's charity club, the Colleagues, whose good causes ranged from raising funds for the Baron House, a home for troubled women to building care centers for battered children. Every May, they organized a big clothes sale, their "glamour-clothes sale", as they called it. They sold their clothes, movie stars donated their gowns, and the fair was held in the famous Bel Air mansion where the "Beverly Hillbillies" television series was shot. Without calling into question the legitimacy and sincerity of their charity work, it can be said that membership of the Colleagues was reserved to an élite network of chic wealthy ladies and celebrities, identified primarily by their social rank. The Reagans grew closer to Harriet and Armand Deutsch, a man who had made his money in commerce and was becoming a mogul in the more celebrated field of motion pictures, where he could translate his riches into fame and glamour; Lee and Walter Annenberg, the publication czar who launched *TV Guide* and *Seventeen*; Betty and William Wilson, whose money came from his father's oil-equipment manufacturing business, etc. The Colleagues limited its number to 65 women. Nancy also spent a lot of time with two other women who belonged to what was referred to in the press as "the Group", a sort of unofficial subdivision of the Colleagues, gathering close friends: Marion Jorgensen, whose husband, Earle M. Jorgensen, had founded the eponymous steel company, and Betsy Bloomingdale, wife of Alfred Bloomingdale, the founder of Diners Club, one of the first credit cards operations, and an heir to the New York popular Bloomingdale department store fortune. Betsy would soon become Nancy's closest friend and confidante. She was an elegant, vivacious, fun-loving lady, the fashion plate in the Group, who took an immense pleasure helping Nancy with her image, advising her on choosing clothes when they went shopping together in Beverly Hills, guiding her on social codes of entertainment and good taste in decoration. Betsy had studied art and possessed a rare artistic talent that she had expressed in collecting pieces and decorating her home which Nancy compared to an art gallery with brilliant *savoir faire*. They would lunch together in the most stylish restaurants, patronize the most sophisticated designers, attend the same fashionable beauty parlors... Betsy exerted some kind of fascination for Nancy when she told her about her extravagant lifestyle, from shopping week-ends in Paris to compelling purchases of the latest designer dresses. Through Betsy's friendship, Nancy enlarged her *beau monde* circle. She was introduced to Jerome "Jerry" Zipkin, the son of Annette Goldstein and David Zipkin, a real estate multimillionaire. Jerry owned whole blocks of apartment buildings on Park Avenue in Manhattan. He was a refined gracious person, possessed an impressive artistic culture, claiming one of the most important private art collections in California. He befriended Somerset Maugham, the British author. According to the writer's biographer Ted Morgan, Maugham had based Elliot Templeton, the snobbish character of *The Razor's Edge* on Zipkin. The Group also included the wives of some of Ronnie's political connections: Virginia Tuttle, a former school teacher, who had co-founded the Los Angeles County Museum of Art and the Music Center. She lived in Hancock Park with Holmes, her husband, the magnate of Ford and Lincoln Mercury dealerships, who appeared to be one of the 30 or so powerful men who secretly ran Los Angeles. Jean Smith, the wife of a prominent lawyer who would later become Ronnie's personal attorney, William French Smith, was the latest member of the Group.

Though he was anything but sophisticated, Ronnie supported his wife in her pursuit of successful people and he kept telling her she looked better and better as if to encourage her in her desire to climb up the social ladder.

In addition to hosting and starring the General Electric (G. E.) TV show, Ronnie was in charge of promoting the corporation and its products all around the United States. In the eight years he spent in the company, he traveled several hundred thousand miles, covering the country from West to East, North to South, several times, addressing countless civic clubs, businesses and organizations, visiting 139 G. E. plants across 38 states, and meeting 250,000 of their employees. As the company's goodwill ambassador, Ronald had his house become itself a showcase for G. E as a gift. It was supplied with the latest electrical gadgets and appliances available. "It'll have everything electric but a chair", Ronnie had joked as his house was turned into the most electric home in the whole nation.[19] As he was on the road – Ronald spent the equivalent of two full years away from "home", crisscrossing America – the couple exchanged a rather voluminous correspondence that reflects the deep sentiments they both sincerely felt for each other. They had got into the habit of opening or signing the letters with funny nicknames, such as "Daddie Poo Pants" and "Mommie Poo Pants". Ronnie also used to send Nancy a lot of telegrams while he was traveling, which revealed how hard it was for him to be separated from home and the family.

- What am I doing here when I want to be there, I miss you & love you.
- Why is it I don't get around to speaking my mind more often like how much I love you and how lost I'd be without you.
- How come it doesn't get any easier, I miss you very much probably because I love you very much.[20]

Nevertheless, significantly enough, the job had made the Reagans wealthy and that financial security had changed their lives through the years. Ronnie also recognized that despite the moments of solitude, he loved being the voice of G. E. Naturally gifted at communication, projecting constant enthusiasm and optimism, he appeared as the company's ideal messenger delivering simple but powerful speeches about the greatness of America, which G. E. was proud to symbolize.

Most importantly, the experience had led to Ronnie's political conversion and growing involvement in state and federal affairs. He had joined the company in 1954 as a Roosevelt Democrat. He left it in 1962 as a staunch Republican. In between, he had revealed a facet of his conservative leanings as a Democrat by supporting Dwight Eisenhower both in 1952 and 1956 and campaigning for Richard Nixon against John F. Kennedy in 1960. Different factors explain this evolution. More than one critic have attributed it to the ambitious Nancy, as she had been cast in the conservative mold of her stepfather, but it would be wrong to over-exaggerate her influence. She had endorsed Dr. Loyal's position out of mimesis rather than sheer conviction. All she wanted, she said, was to support her husband. And she devoted her time encouraging him in any enterprise he would commit himself in, political or not. "I've read that I'm the one who's pushing Ronnie politically. That's just not true. If Ronnie were selling shoes, I'd be out pushing shoes," she would insist.[21] Ronnie certainly admired his father-in-law's conservative views and in that sense Nancy became an indirect influence. Would

---

[19] Leamer, op. cit., p. 177.
[20] *I Love You*, op. cit., p. 71.
[21] Melinda Beck, et. al., "The Woman Behind Reagan", *Newsweek*, April 28, 1980, p. 38.

he have ever become a Republican had he never met Nancy? His political conservatism also originated from his experiences as president of the Screen Actors Guild but it was his years with G. E. that had considerable impact. It put him in contact with the world of corporate executives with whom he polished his speaking style by defending the virtues of big business and the vices of big government. He denounced the growing and detrimental interference of Washington technocracy in the free enterprise system and in the every day lives of American citizens. In the late 1950s, he attacked the welfare state and government choices so vehemently that it almost cost him his job. The Tennessee Valley Authority (TVA), one of the New Deal large-scale projects, became his favorite target. The problem was the TVA was a G. E. client that returned $50,000 in government contracts. Inevitably, the company's executives took a dim view of Ronnie's growing partisanship and feared the potential risk for their business operations. The political tone of his speeches and television show eventually soured too many people at G. E. and, in 1962, the program was canceled. During that period, Ronnie realized his ideas were at variance with his Democratic Party affiliation and consequently in 1962, he made the logical decision of siding with the Republicans.

In the summer of 1964, it became more and more obvious that President Johnson would win the presidential election. Democrats portrayed Barry Goldwater, the Republican candidate, not just as an ultra conservative but as a dangerous extremist. In California, Ronald Reagan co-chaired the "Citizens for Goldwater-Miller" campaign which he marked with one of the landmark speeches in his political career. Holmes Tuttle, one of the Republican Party's biggest fundraisers, had asked him to fill in for Goldwater who, because of a scheduling problem, could not speak at the $1,000-a-plate dinner held at the Cocoanut Grove nightclub in the Ambassador Hotel, downtown Los Angeles. His passionate "A Time for Choosing" speech, televised statewide, was such a hit that Tuttle had it re-aired on the national NBC network so that one week before the election, on October 27, 1964, Reagan's message was delivered nationwide. It was a simple but eloquent and powerful message, that went straight to the hearts of the audience. "You and I have a rendezvous with destiny", he concluded, paradoxically borrowing the words from his former hero FDR. "We can preserve for our children this, the last best hope of man on earth, or we can sentence them to take the first step into a thousand years of darkness."

"If we fail, at least let our children and our children's children say of us we justified our brief moment here. We did all we could do."[22]

The apocalyptic anti-Communist rhetoric and the vibrant defense of free market economy did not reverse the national pro-Democrat trend as Goldwater suffered one of the most crushing defeats in America's presidential history. President Johnson boasted 43 million popular votes. Goldwater only received a humiliating 27 million and won only six states. Yet the response to Reagan's speech added $1 million in contributions to the coffers of the Republican Party. In addition, the Goldwater debacle had the positive effect of highlighting Reagan's qualities. Columnist David S. Broder of the *Washington Post* called it "the most successful national political debut since William Jennings Bryan electrified the 1896 Democratic convention with his 'Cross of Gold' speech."[23]

Soon Ronald thought he had stayed long enough behind the scenes and the success of his speech convinced him that he had to pitch himself into the political arena. Two months later, in January 1965, Holmes Tuttle, Henry Salvatori, the finance chairman of the California Republican Party, and A. C. "Cy" Rubel, chairman of the board of Union Oil, decided to approach Reagan about running for the governorship of California. After all, he would not be the first actor to endorse a political career. Two years before, his friend George Murphy, an ex Hollywood star, had defeated Pierre Salinger, who had been President Kennedy's press secretary, for a California U. S. Senate seat. Reagan also knew that, though he no longer shared her liberal convictions, Helen Gahagan Douglas, a former Broadway actress and opera diva, as early as 1944, had been the first non politico to run for the United States House of Representatives and win. So why not him? It was clear that "the Speech" had now established him as a national political figure. Backed by 41 influential friends from the California business community who formed "The Friends of Ronald Reagan", the former Captain Abbott who, following the end of his G. E. contract, had been hosting *Death Valley Days*, a syndicated television program sponsored by U.S. Borax, quickly agreed to become a candidate but waited till January 1966 to announce it officially.

When incumbent governor Edmund Gerald "Pat" Brown heard the news, he did not take it seriously. For him, Reagan was another opportunistic right-wing lunatic trying to get a name in the political field because he had failed in Hollywood. Moreover, Brown's clan maneuvered the opinion by associating Ronald and his committee of rich people with the racist extreme right-wing John

---

[22] Bill Adler, *Ronnie and Nancy: A very Special Love Story* (New York: Crown Publishers, 1985), p. 119.
[23] Kati Marion, *Hidden Power: Presidential Marriages that Shaped our Recent History* (New York: Pantheon Books, 2001), p. 251

Birch Society. True, the Society had pervaded the Republican Party in Southern California. But Reagan brushed aside accusations with the back of his hand: "Any members of the Society who support me", he said unequivocally, "will be buying *my* philosophy. I won't be buying theirs."[24] Brown, who remained condescending and derisive, ignored the Reagan candidacy and focused his campaign vilifying the other Republican candidate George Christopher, the former mayor of San Francisco. His judgment could not have been more misguided since it was Ronnie who won the Republican nomination. with a princely 64% of the vote. Now the campaign could move into high gear.

Nancy was rather timorous at first and did not play much of a role. Her reaction was rather ambivalent. She had written to a friend: "It boggles the mind but maybe it'll get me out of the carpool."[25] As the campaign progressed, she gradually found it exhilarating. "If I never imagined myself the wife of a political leader," she wrote in *Nancy*, "I certainly never pictured myself on the campaign trail. Yet it has been one of the most interesting, revealing, and rewarding experiences I've ever had. Yes, it's tiring but I wouldn't have traded it for anything."[26] She was to stand by her man and project the proper image of the beautiful wife and perfect family to the public, which was the political role she preferred to play and at which she excelled. But that was just the easy part of the job.

As she was required to participate more actively, she felt it hard to overcome her shyness and insecurity. When Ronnie's staff asked her to make speeches, she was initially reticent because she felt uncomfortable with crowds. She would eventually work out a compromise by replacing speeches with question-and-answer public meetings and interviews with the press. She appeared at countless ladies' groups and fundraisers. She was friendly with people most of the time except when it came to personal questions, which she would deliberately parry with a frown.

Another difficulty she had to face was criticism, which she simply could not tolerate. She was all the more upset if she felt it could hurt her husband. Yes, she admitted later, it was hard to keep her self control. She was shocked by the ferocity of the media against public figures in general, politicians in particular, especially during an electoral race. As she campaigned with Ronnie, she always made sure to be at his side, listening to his speeches attentively with her head slightly tilted, her hazel eyes wide open and her face glowing in total awe of him.

---

[24] Leighton, op. cit., p. 98.
[25] Mary Linehan, "Nancy Reagan", in Robert P., Watson, ed. *American First Ladies* (Pasadena, Ca.: Salem Press, 2002), p. 301.
[26] *Nancy*, op. cit., p. 144.

Reporters, both male and female, soon made fun of the worshipful way she used to stare at her husband. They derisively called it "the Gaze", "the Look", "the Stare", to denounce what they considered a calculated and hypocritical picture, "prima-facie evidence of a Goodie Two-Shoes phoniness."[27] Lou Cannon, a *Washington Post* correspondent, defined the look as "a kind of transfixed adoration more appropriate to a witness of the Virgin Birth." A *Chicago Tribune* writer described the scene as follows: "Her eyes sparkle as if she were in some kind of trance. Hearing a one-liner for the one-hundredth time, she laughs on cue and then resumes her adoring gaze." The criticism even came from her own circle of friends as one said: "Nancy, people just don't *believe* it when you look at Ronnie that way—as though you're saying, 'He's my hero.'" "But he *is* my hero", she snapped back.[28] Nancy invariably adopted the same loving focus on her husband, no matter how many times she had heard the same speech or the same anecdotes. And she remained the same throughout Ronnie's career. "Mrs. Reagan gazes at her husband like he's a hot fudge sundae and she hasn't eaten all day", wrote Jill Gerston fourteen years later.[29]

Nancy defended and protected her Ronnie at all times, almost excessively. According to Paul Beck, a *Los Angeles Times* reporter who would later become Reagan's press secretary, she was "a tigress protecting her favorite cub."[30] In private, he called her "mommy" and he was her "Daddy", a word she had seldom dared to pronounce ever before. In the campaign, they worked as a team. He could not run for office without her, not only because it was traditionally the rule in politics but simply because he wanted her close. Her presence and support were as precious as diamonds. He had faith in her and she had faith in him. And she soon revealed herself as a born politician. Her role grew as she gained confidence and participated in meetings of the campaign team as they talked over strategic matters, raising the right issues, asking the tough questions and making sensible suggestions. She could make decisions too. As her husband's protector, she kept an attentive eye on Ronnie's personnel, who was going to be around him, where, and so on. She somewhat supervised the staff operations. Her obvious political skills were sharpened during that period. They would be refined with time.

Candidate Reagan led his campaign as Mr. Everyman, middle-class, baseball fan, a typically western horse lover, who resented higher taxes, the ever higher crime rate, the growing welfare dependency, or the utopian counter-culture alternative lifestyle. But his discourse was not that of an embittered person. No,

---

[27] Kurt Andersen, "Co-Star at the White House", *Time*, 14 January 1985, p. 6.
[28] « California's Leading Lady », *Look*, October 31, 1967, p. 40.
[29] Jill Gerston, "The Stargazer", in *The Philadelphia Inquirer*, 13 October, 1980, p. D1.
[30] Leamer, op. cit., p. 198.

his optimism predominated the tone of his speeches. His Good Guy image, such as the one he used to play on television, was polished by two professional political image makers Stuart "Stu" Spencer and William Roberts who had been hired at $50,000 a year. Reagan's communicative qualities lay not so much in the content of his message as in its form. He focused all of his attention on Governor Brown with a series of one-liners that kept audiences laughing: "Keeping up with Governor Brown's promises", he once said, "is like reading *Playboy* magazine while your wife turns the pages."

Another: "The Governor talks about *his* dams and *his* lakes and *his* reservoirs; you have the feeling that when he leaves office he'll take them with him."

The humor could turn more sarcastic when it came to personal allusions: "Well, he's good to his family.... He's put a lot of relatives on the payroll."

He lashed out against the economic problems and high cost of living: "You ladies know that if you stand at the supermarket these days, it's cheaper to eat money."

Or: "Do you remember back in the days when you thought that *nothing* could replace the dollar? Today it practically has!"[31]

Brown, on the other hand, kept highlighting Ronnie's lack of experience, comparing him to an airline pilot telling his passengers that it was his first flight: "But not to worry, I've always had a very active interest in the field of aviation."[32] The governor, who was sure to be reelected as a Democrat in a Democratic state, also insisted on Reagan's inability to reach out to poor people and minorities: "There is not a black, a Chicano, a Jew, a poor man, or even a middle-class working American who has Reagan's ear", he said."[33] But in March 1966, riots broke out in Watts. Brown's rivals seized the opportunity to remind the population that during the black ghetto's upheaval that had killed thirty-four people in August the year before, the governor had been on vacation abroad. It had been a bad year for Democrats as student anti-Vietnam War demonstrations at the University of Berkeley had spawned a conservative backlash.

As the general election approached, the campaign became increasingly sour and exacerbated hostilities between each clan. In August, the prospect of a Reagan victory appeared distinctly possible as a Gallup poll placed Reagan eleven points ahead of his opponent. The Democrats' response took the form of a 29-page report with the scathing title: "Ronald Reagan, Extremist Collaborator, an Exposé." But the excoriating paper proved a complete waste of effort. Governor Brown would not beat Reagan as he had beaten Richard Nixon four years before.

---

[31] Stewart Alsop, quoted in Adler, op. cit., p. 124.
[32] Leighton, op. cit., p. 98.
[33] *Ibid.*, p. 94.

There would be no third term. Reagan's victory was a landslide, collecting 3,742,913 votes and winning 53 counties, against Brown's miserable 2,749,174 and 5.

Part III

Sacramento: The Road
to Washington D. C.

On January 2, 1967, one minute after 12:00 A.M., Ronald Reagan, fifty-five years old, was sworn in as governor of California, the most populous state in the union. The reason for such an odd hour was Nancy's belief in astrology. She had talked to Washington, D. C., soothsayer Jeane Dixon to find the most favorable time. Every now and then, she would resort to the occult to sort things out, arrange and rearrange schedules, even at the last minute. Most of the time Ronnie did not mind or did not know. He was aware that she believed in the power of planets and stars to influence or predict the course of events but pleaded in her favor as he knew that all was meant for his safety and well-being. The constant attention he received from her filled him with joy and made him thrive. The Reagan staff, in charge of executing her decisions promptly, had a less appreciative opinion.

The early inauguration hour also had the political advantage of preventing Brown from appointing more judges before leaving office.

The official ceremony took place in the Capitol rotunda with a beaming Nancy at Ronnie's side, looking tearfully and triumphantly at her husband as he swore his oath of office. Ronnie opened his inaugural speech by thanking his old friend-actor-senator George Murphy: "Well, Murph, here we are again on 'the Late, Late Show'." Murphy had played Ronnie's father in *This Is the Army* (1943) and co-starred with Nancy in *Talk About a Stranger* (1952). Like Ronnie, he had turned from Democrat to Republican. The new governor also acknowledged the presence of Reverend Donn Moomaw of Bel Air Presbyterian Church. He went on with an outline of his short-term and mid-term plans for his administration, assuring his audience, all eyes and all ears, of his whole-hearted commitment to the prosperity of the blue and gold state.

After the official celebration came festivities. The buffet supper Betty Wilson had organized in the Governor's mansion and the subsequent Inaugural Ball were dazzling displays of elegance and glamour. In her sparkling white beaded dress designed by James Galanos, wearing real diamond and emerald ear-rings, Nancy looked much younger than her age, forty-five. As the tradition goes, the First Couple opened the dance and were soon joined by the whole California glitterati. They all had a sumptuous night, but Ronnie and Nancy certainly enjoyed it more than everyone else.

A new phase in their lives began. United for life, very much in love with each other, they felt confident about their future and ready to meet the new challenges facing their private and public lives.

Yet the difficulties arrived probably sooner than they had expected. Settling down in the unfamiliar settings of Sacramento was no easy accomplishment. Children were the first major concern as they had to find them new schools. Little Ron was reluctant to leave John Dye, his school in Bel Air, but there was no better solution than enrolling him at Brookfield, a private elementary school in Sacramento, which would allow him to live at home. There he received basic education and developed creative arts, a minor compensation for a nine-year-old. Patti was sent to Orme High School in Arizona. Dr. Loyal and DeeDee had recommended it as it offered an unusual curriculum combining academic classes and more practical outdoor ranch activities. She would ride horses and take care of the cattle, as a real cowgirl. Patti liked the school but, aged fourteen, she soon became a major problem in the family. She was no longer a good little mommy's girl and had started to reveal her independent and rebellious nature on different circumstances. Worst of all, no doubt, had been her defiant decision to wear a Pat Brown T-shirt during her father's campaign for the governorship. She could not have hurt her parents' feelings more, and knew it.

Nancy's most serious source of annoyance appeared as she realized their residence was inappropriate for the governor of the richest state in the nation. It was rundown, noisy, dark and inhospitable. The building, an 1879 four-story Victorian mansion, was located right in the middle of the capital, on a major thoroughfare, overlooking a gas station and a motel and backing up to the American Legion Hall. The contrast with her quiet Palisades House was striking: no patio, no flowers, colors or light. No ocean view. No quiet starlit nights. If the new place was a house, for Nancy it was certainly not a home. Under pressure from her, Ronnie raised the issue with his advisers who warned him against having a new house built. His predecessor had already taken steps to get a new residence. They had found an architect, he had drawn plans but eventually the state legislature had rejected the project. There were other priorities and the cost was too high.

Another change Nancy found hard to adjust to was living in a small town, far from Los Angeles. She missed her well-heeled friends Betsy, Mary Jane and the rest of the Group. She missed the charity fairs and balls and luncheons and shopping. "Thank heavens we can escape to Beverly Hills on the weekends," she said to a journalist, as reported by Stephen Birmingham in *California Rich*. Every now and then, she relieved her boredom with trips to L. A., lunching and gossiping at the Bistro in Beverly Hills, going on a buying spree at Gucci's Italian fashion store on Rodeo Drive, watching a show... She felt a compelling need to fly south because "no one in Sacramento can do hair." Also, shopping in Sacramento at I. Magnin's was fine, but ill-adapted to her tastes. "Here everything is scaled down for these Valley farm women" she was reported to have said.[1]

Still, real life was in Sacramento, for better or for worse. For her husband's fifty-sixth birthday, in February, she decided to have the governor's drab office in the State Capitol redecorated and there was no time to lose in one month! She put in red carpeting, repaired and reupholstered the old leather couch, stained the fading yellow wooden walls brown and covered them with old English horse prints from their Palisades house. She also bought her husband a large antique desk that was more suitable for a governor. Ronnie was moved by his wife's birthday gift and thanked her dearly and praised her and told her how much he loved her. Stimulated by all the compliments she was receiving, from Ronnie but also from friends and visitors, she went on to renovate all the hallways and rooms of the old edifice, one after the other. Like Jackie Kennedy, to whom she liked being compared, she enjoyed decoration and had an indisputable talent for choosing the right material and the right colors for the right place. The reception room in particular was highly valued. She had taken down the ugly nineteenth century leather on the walls and replaced it with burlap. To adorn the recovered walls, she hung up some old but valuable historic prints of Sacramento, San Francisco and Los Angeles, pictures of early nineteenth century legislators and views of the building of the capitol. As a caring First Lady, she invited local artists to hang their pictures in turn, for a permanent exhibition.

But Nancy's major problem was not settled yet and as days went by, her feeling of repulsion for the house she lived in kept growing. There was no way Ronnie could get her to change her mind. She considered the dilapidated mansion

---

[1] Laurence Leamer, *Make-Believe: The Story of Nancy & Ronald Reagan* (New York: Harper and Row, 1983), p. 211.

a firetrap, unsafe for the family. There were seven fireplaces in the house but none of them could be lit. It was prohibited by law because they could set the house ablaze! In addition, the mansion had no fire escapes. Then one afternoon, when Skipper was at home, the fire alarms went off for a practice exercise. Nancy led him down the stairs outside where they met the fire marshal. She told the man that it was just impossible to open the windows in her son's room. What could he do in case of fire? "Well, Mrs. Reagan", he replied, "tell him to pull one of the drawers out of the bureau dresser... Tell him to hold it out in front of him and, run toward the window, break it, and climb out. He'll be safe on the roof outside."[2]

For the perfectionist and protective mother, that was the last straw. Seething with rage, she undertook an immediate house-hunt on her own, regardless of state legislators. After a few days of careful exploration around the city, she eventually found what she had been looking for, a house spacious enough, quiet enough and comfortable enough for a governor's family. It was a twelve-room, two story Tudor-style house located in a peaceful suburban neighborhood area on Forty-Fifth Street. Here they would no longer be disturbed by the endless rumble of trucks and buses, and no gas station or motels were on view. In April 1967, only four months after their arrival in Sacramento, they moved in. They rented the house $1,250 per month. Now the governor was glad to see his wife smile again. Her little boy was out of danger and in their huge backyard, where they had installed a tree house and a swing, he could invite his friends to play. The swimming-pool was a popular place for children and for the governor's guests during barbecues and parties.

But the new residence provoked a storm of protest. First of all, there were charges of racism, to which Nancy responded by hiring an MGM publicity agent for her staff. Ronnie's aides were baffled too. They thought the move out of the city was as a political faux-pas, a "political suicide" and would lead to confusion and contempt, which might compromise the chances of future political races. And indeed there was quite a bit of public exasperation. Politicians and their wives blamed Nancy for putting on queenly airs. How come His Excellency's Lady refused to live in the mansion that had served the Browns and generations of governors and their families? Nancy felt hurt when some people started to dub her "Queen Nancy." Finding the accusations unfair and to deflect the flow of indignation, she invited the wives of state legislatures on tours of the old "Victorian-ugly" mansion so they could see how seedy and unsafe the place was.

---

[2] Bill Adler, *Ronnie and Nancy : A very Special Love Story* (New York: Crown Publishers, 1985), p. 131.

She also organized poolside parties in the new estate with old friends like Jack Benny, Danny Thomas and Red Skelton as entertainers.

Nancy, and eventually Ronnie, disliked the old governor's house so much that they, Nancy, launched a campaign to build a new, safe official Governor's Mansion, worthy of the name. Money would be raised through public subscription. The Reagans found a proper place in a suburban area, overlooking the American River. The land would cost no money to the taxpayer as it was donated to the state.

Meanwhile, Nancy complained that the governor had to pay the rent on the Forty-Fifth Street house. "I can't believe we had to rent it with our own money," she later explained to a reporter. "Wouldn't you think that the state would provide a residence for the governor and his family? When I go to other states and see how the governors live, I'm embarrassed; we're an important and powerful state, and deserve an official residence."[3]

She also called for public donations of antiques that she could use to furnish her twelve roomed Tudor House until the new official mansion was built.

Two years after they had moved into their rented house, the owner asked them to move or buy the house, on expiration of the lease. The governor's Kitchen Cabinet and good friends, the Tuttles, Bloomingdales, Salvatoris and Co. purchased it for $150,000 and leased it again to the Reagans, for the same $1,250 a month.

The succession of complaints and desires on the part of the state's First Family, the First Lady quite particularly, provoked vehement protest among people and in the press. There was suspicion that her acquisition of furniture was for herself and not for the state. Jesse Unruh, the Speaker of the California Assembly, who was running against Reagan in 1970, was the most virulent and led the pack of detractors. The criticism reached such a point that she furiously called a press conference, her first one, to deny the charges. She took advantage of the occasion to thank donators and congratulate herself for her decoration work: "Frankly, I'm proud of what I've done. I wanted to get a good start collecting things for the mansion, having them donated to the state, the same as they did for the White House. The people who donated to the White House received a pat on the back. The people who donated here deserve the same thanks."[4]

Political opponents were persuaded that the wealthy friends who had purchased the house would benefit from small special interest compensations. So criticism also targeted Ronald himself, even on such petty political questions.

---

[3] Kitty Kelley, *Nancy Reagan: The Unauthorized Biography* (New York: Pocket Star Books, 1991), p. 153.

[4] *Ibid.*, p. 155.

Right from the beginning of his mandate, at his very first press conference, he had to be on the defensive and repudiated the unpleasant questions. Fortunately, he never lost his self-control and knew how to handle the most violent attacks: "I'd always heard a new governor was given a bit of a honeymoon by the press. Fellows, if this is a honeymoon, I've been sleeping alone."[5] Nancy could not stand seeing her husband deprecated or sneered at. Once she called Otis Chandler, the *Los Angeles Times* publisher, to complain about a Paul Conrad cartoon that had ridiculed the governor of California. She judged it disrespectful to the man and the function. Another time, as she was on a plane with Nancy Reynolds, her press secretary, two men sitting behind them happened to be running down Ronald Reagan and his budget cuts. "I could see the blood rising in Nancy's face", Reynolds recalled, "Suddenly she flips back the seat, turns around and says, 'That's my husband you're talking about and that budget is what this state needs.' Nancy didn't shout but she was very firm. 'You don't know what you're saying. He's going on television tonight, and if you watch him you'll learn the real story of the budget.'"[6]

The truth was, the Reagans were considered as an anomaly in Sacramento. Their lifestyle certainly was. Almost every Friday evening they would set off to their Palisades house and not return until Monday morning. They would rest and relax, away from the political turbulences of the capital. Nancy would sometimes return shopping at Amelia Gray's, her favorite store in Beverly Hills. But in a small town like Sacramento everyone knew everyone and everyone was a politician or revolved around the political sphere. It was hard to understand that the governor did not go out after hours and relax over a long drink in a popular bar, talking more freely about current events with some friends or associates. But Ronnie's idea of a perfect evening, like Nancy's, was more traditional, reflecting a fifties' Ozzie and Harriet family flavor, that is being just together, eating dinner from their silver trays and watching their favorite show on television.

This need for privacy, which was an essential part of their life, was interpreted as a sense of aloofness, just as the rented house was.

And it did not improve their relationships with the press. Mrs. Reagan's, in particular, became increasingly strained. This was a paradox because she was making real efforts to cultivate a positive image with reporters, as shown in the following lines from *Look*: "At 44, Nancy Reagan looks like a Republican version

---

[5] Adler, op. cit., p. 134.
[6] Nancy Reynolds, quoted in Kati Marion, *Hidden Power: Presidential Marriages that Shaped our Recent History* (New York: Pantheon Books, 2001), p. 253; Nancy Reagan, with William Novak, *My Turn: the Memoirs of Nancy Reagan* (New York: Random House, 1989), pp. 141-142.

of Jacqueline Kennedy. She has the same spare figure, the same air of immaculate chic. I had the impression," wrote the reporter, "that even in the high wind, her short, reddish-brownish-goldish hair would stay in precise order. . . Her handsome face, her large eyes, and full mouth give away whatever she is feeling at all times."[7]

In the spring, she granted an interview to essayist and novelist Joan Didion, then a columnist for the *Saturday Evening Post*. Mrs. Reagan received her on her Sacramento estate and showed her around the house. The two women had got along very well. The Q and A game was conducted in a most civil and pleasant way. Some days later, as she was flying to Chicago, she found the *Post* on board and eagerly leafed through the magazine until she found the right page. What she read left her flabbergasted. The interview had been processed into a scathing profile entitled "Pretty Nancy", portraying the First Lady as an insincere daydreaming woman, constantly playacting in a superficial world. "Nancy Reagan has an interested smile," Didion wrote, "the smile of a good wife, a good mother, a good hostess, the smile of someone who grew up in comfort and went to Smith College and has a father who is a distinguished neurosurgeon (her father's entry in the 1966-67 *Who's Who* runs nine lines longer than her husband's) and a husband who is a definition of Nice Guy, not to mention Governor of California, the smile of a woman who seems to be playing out some middle-class American woman's daydream, circa 1948. The set for this daydream is perfectly dressed, every detail correct. This is the rented house on 45th Street. . . .

"There are two dogs, named Lady and Fuzzy, and there are two children, named Pattie and Ronnie. Pattie, 15, is described as artistic, and she goes to a boarding school in Arizona. Ronnie, 10, is referred to as a regular boy, and he goes to a private school in Sacramento. He is also referred to as 'the Skipper.'" And to crown it all, Didion had mocked her smile as "a study in frozen insecurity."[8] It seemed that every word in the article was meant to hurt, and did. Embittered by such acid-tongued prose, feeling that she had been trapped, Nancy grew increasingly wary of the press. She surrounded herself with a team of reliable supervisors in charge of controlling interviews beforehand. But sometimes, at least once, as Sally Quinn, from the *Washington Post* recalls, her caution developed into vigorous rage: "She gripped both my shoulders while she chewed me out about a comment I'd made on TV a few weeks before. I could feel that grip for a long time."[9] Indeed it seemed that women reporters were the fiercest of Nancy's detractors. She overtly affirmed: "My life began when I

---

[7] « California's Leading Lady », *Look*, October 31, 1967, p. 40.
[8] Joan Didion, « Pretty Nancy », *Saturday Evening Post*, June 1, 1968, p. 20.
[9] Marion, op. cit., p. 254.

married Ronnie. My life fell into place when I married him. He gave me security and peace of mind, and love. I wasn't looking for anything more. I had it."[10] In the early days of the women's liberation movement, those candid words were interpreted as sheer provocation and generated negative comments around the nation. How could a state First Lady be so out of touch with reality? Did she know nothing about the changing gender roles, women as equal partners with their husbands? Didion's stab in the back article had been a product of that new culture.

After Ronald's sweeping victory over Brown in 1966, Holmes Tuttle and some other advisors were persuaded that the man they had led to the head of the state was of the stuff presidents were made of and time had come to make a try. Under their pressure, Ronald entered the race for the 1968 Republican presidential nomination against Governor Nelson Rockefeller and Eisenhower's vice-president Richard Milhous Nixon. Bill Clark and some other aides had argued against the nomination but to no avail. It all happened so rapidly that even Nancy did not know. She heard the news on the radio and was angered not to have been kept informed. She even panicked when, on the night of California's primary, TV and radio stations released the news of Robert Kennedy's assassination. The young senator, JFK's brother, had just won the nomination for the Democratic Party.

The Republican National Convention that was held in Miami Beach in August 1968 gave Nixon a handy victory on the first roll-call vote. Reagan received 182 delegate votes, coming third behind Rockefeller. The mediocre, almost humiliating, results proved that Ronald's campaign had been too brief and poorly organized. It also proved that Ronald was not yet ready for Pennsylvania Avenue. And the greatest lesson of it all was that Ronnie would never again make such major—as well as minor—decisions without consulting his wife.

During his tenure as governor, Ronald Reagan was confronted with a series of major problems. To begin with, he was furious to discover that his predecessor had left him a $200,000,000 budget deficit. The tax cuts the staunch anti-communist, anti-bureaucrat and free enterprise advocate had promised during the campaign could not be realized. More, he had to propose some controversial proposals to balance the budget. By far the most unpopular was the introduction of tuition fees in hitherto free state colleges and universities.

In the tumultuous sixties, Reagan and the unruly world of education were in permanent confrontation. One of his first decisions had been to get rid of the University of California's liberal president Clark Kerr, whom he considered responsible for the growing "anarchy" on campus. He stood firm on law and order

[10] Adler, op. cit., p. 136.

and spared no effort to quell students' protest strikes as they marched in the streets, burning the American flag and their draft documents or denouncing the bombing in North Vietnam. A strong anti-war movement had pervaded young America. People's Park in Berkeley became the symbol of the culture clash between adults and the young, between power holders and freedom fighters, between Reagan and students. The park had been converted from a parking lot into a community park by radical activists and long-haired marijuana-smoking hippies who had planted flowers and "improved" the space. Not sharing the same sense of taste in landscaping, the authorities soon decided to put up a fence around the university-owned land. Resistance organized itself and several thousand young people flocked towards the park in support. Unable to contain this unruly crowd, the governor mobilized the National Guard. In a few hours, the place was turned into an odd but violent battlefield. Bricks were thrown, shotguns fired and teargas sprayed on the campus from helicopters. One protester was killed, another blinded. A policeman was stabbed and over sixty people injured.

To her parents' amazement and incomprehension, Patti Reagan herself joined the young people's revolt. She had suffered through all these events while she was at Orme School and once at the University of Southern California, the rebellious teenager plunged headlong into the current of counterculture and, like most of her fellow-students, became a fervent opponent of the Vietnam War. Meanwhile, her mother Nancy, like her father Ronald, judged it would be immoral for the American nation to pull out of Vietnam. At the Woodstock pop festival in 1969, Joan Baez mocked the governor of California as "Ray-gun" and blasted him for his vocal support of the war. Dan McCabe, a friend of Ron Jr. at Harvard, later said of Reagan: "There was such animosity toward him then. It was part of the culture. He was the guy they loved to hate on California campuses."[11] Even Patti saw her father as "the enemy". This disagreement within the First Family perfectly exemplified the generation gap.

Ronald Reagan also encountered problems at the very heart of his administration when it was revealed that a few members of his staff, some respectable married men, had been involved in a torrid homosexual party. The orgy, Reagan was told, had taken place in a cabin at Lake Tahoe. As the news started to spread, most of the accused resigned over the following days. To make the sordid episode worse, director of communications Lyn Nofziger leaked the story to the press which was too pleased to detail the facts in its columns and charge Reagan himself for covering up the scandal. Nancy, who had long been irritated by Nofziger's "rumpled appearance and bearing", lack of style,

---

[11] Leamer, op. cit., p. 242.

inappropriate choice of clothes – crumpled suits, ill-matched colors – by his infinite ego and, above all by the way he had prompted rather than assisted her husband during the campaign, put all the blame on the man. Six months later, under the First Lady's pressure, he was fired.[12]

As governor, Ronald had to make terribly tough decisions about the life or death of individuals. In April 1967, he confirmed the execution of Aaron Mitchell who had been on death row for two years at San Quentin Prison for killing a policeman. The night before Mitchell was executed, pro-life protesters kept an all-night vigil outside the Reagans' house, carrying candles and praying for his soul. Nancy had to explain to her intrigued little boy the reason for the peculiar gathering. She tried to tell him with simple words that as the supreme authority of the state, his dad had the power to pardon the man but had followed his conscience and maintained the death penalty. His decision reflected the will of the great majority of Californians who considered the sentence a deterrent to murder.

As First Lady of California, Nancy traveled around the state on official duties, visiting schools or public establishments, participating in charity programs, fundraising activities, or attending cultural events. She made a point of making the rounds of hospitals, meeting young as well as elderly patients, handicapped people as well as little babies and their mothers. Probably because she had been a nurse's aide and undoubtedly owing to Dr. Loyal's influence, she had always attached great importance to the hospital world. In the course of her frequent visits, she became particularly interested in one program developed at Pacific State Hospital by Sargent Shriver. The "Foster Grandparents" principle consisted in bringing older people who were ready to help into close contact with mentally retarded children who need extra attention and affection. The two-year experiment was producing excellent results but was too small and very poorly funded. Nancy made it into her pet project and lobbied her husband to raise money. It was gradually expanded to all state hospitals and received more funds as it came under ACTION, the federal volunteer-service agency. The program was started in other states and initiated new networks of relationships including the deaf and juvenile delinquents. On a trip to Australia, Mrs. Reagan presented the program to local medical centers and with her help and advice, a similar version of Foster Grandparents was put on.

As she visited hospitals around the state, she spent much time with wounded veterans. Traveling in Vietnam with an official delegation, she made a point of visiting every hospital sheltering wounded Americans. She confessed that she was

---

[12] Frances Spatz Leighton, *The Search For the Real Nancy Reagan* (New York: Macmillan Publishing Company, 1987), p. 107; Leamer, op. cit., p. 213.

deeply moved by these young people's "acts of bravery" on the front lines. She soon felt concerned about the plight of American POWs in Vietnam and agreed to write a question-and-answer column for the press about their courage and suffering. The only condition was that all the profits from the column were donated to the National League of Families of American Prisoners of War and Missing In Action.

Stories about the Vietnam war and its human consequences always brought tears and sorrow. Yet the moments of sadness were sometimes interrupted by funny episodes that emerged unexpectedly as flashes of relief. Once, as Governor Reagan held a press conference in his office to inform Californians of the creation of the POW-MIA organization by soldiers' wives, his attention was caught by one of the little kids present who was tugging at his pants: "Will you help bring my daddy home?", the frail little voice asked the governor. The scene that occurred in front of TV cameras instantly raised a flow of tears in the viewers' eyes and Ronald himself had to fight to control his emotion. He promised the little boy that he would try his best. A few minutes later, still before the cameras, came another tug from the same little boy: "I have to go to the bathroom," was the new request. All of a sudden, the room was filled with a roar of laughter. The governor took the child's hand and excused himself. The end of the story was not so amusing for the little boy. His father never returned. A few years later, Ronnie and Nancy were glad to hear that his mother had married another POW and the family were all very happy.

Despite her view of the war as a noble and moral endeavor, Nancy was worried about the boys out there, and devoted some of her time to the soldiers' wives and families. She wrote letters and spent time on the phone giving the worried women information about the troops whenever she could, trying to sympathize and comfort them. As prisoners started returning home, the First Couple of California gave four dinners to honor the heroes and their families. Tears and laughter alternated as dramatic stories of torture and life in captivity were told. Two men who had been prisoners in adjoining cells, but had never met, came face to face in the governor's living room and on hearing each other's name, understood they were the closest friends. They had communicated by code-tapping on the cell walls and knew everything about each other's life and family. The scene was an intensely emotional moment which Nancy would often relate later on. She wrote in her 1989 autobiography, *My Turn*, that "the return of the POWs marked the high point of Ronnie's administration."[13]

---

[13] *My Turn*, op. cit., p. 141.

In order to pay for the reelection campaign, the Reagans had sold their Malibu ranch to Twentieth Century Fox for $1,931,000, a good deal compared to the purchasing price of $85,000 in 1951. But nature lover Ronnie missed the peace and quiet of simple outdoor life, riding horses in the wide open California spaces. Though she had been a city-dweller for most of her existence, Nancy had grown into a ranch life lover too and, like Ronnie, she desperately needed an isolated place in which to relax, far away from public scrutiny. In 1968, their good friends the Wilsons bought an undeveloped piece of property in Riverside County where they hosted frequent tailgate parties with the Schreibers, the Smiths and the Reagans. Betty organized Nancy's birthday there every year. They all loved the place so much that each family soon bought adjoining land. The Reagans acquired a 778 acre piece for $347,000. The area was called Rancho California. It had no buildings but the site offered a gorgeous landscape of rolling hills and oak woods hosting an intense wildlife. The word had passed that roads and basic utilities would be extended into the area pretty soon. But as none of these projects seemed to ever materialize, the Wilsons decided to buy an avocado ranch north of Santa Barbara. It was a better served area. The Reagans were often invited and Nancy's birthday parties were transferred there.

The Wilsons then bought a fabulous spread in Mexico. One day Bill Wilson came up with a bright idea that would change Ronnie and Nancy's life for the better. He suggested that they drive to a nearby ranch that was for sale up on a mountaintop from where one had a unique view. The narrow one-laned tortuous road looked, and felt, more like a trail as the car jolted on to the old ranch. Nancy was scared to death and had the feeling of dangling in space when the wheels ran on the edge of steep slopes, dropping abruptly like precipices. But she was brave and patient. Making it eventually to their destination, they discovered a huge wild expanse overgrown with scrub oak and madrone. But behind the oaks, they suddenly looked down on a spread of enchanting rolling meadows spotted with a few sparse farm buildings and in the distance the Pacific Ocean faded away on the blue horizon. The name of the ranch fit the place perfectly, Rancho del Cielo: the Ranch in the Sky in Spanish. It was perched up on a plateau atop a 2,000 foot mountain overlooking the Santa Ynez valley. The property also included a tiny little five-roomed adobe house nestled in a glade. There was a lot of work to do to improve the whole place but Ronnie did not mind the challenge. Nancy was happy to see that Ronnie had found the place he wanted, with no roads and traffic, away from the outside world. They sold Rancho California for $856,000 and acquired the 688-acre Rancho del Cielo for $527,000. From then on, they would drive the 70 miles every free weekend from Sacramento to fix up the old hacienda. With the help of William Barnett, "Barney", his bodyguard, chauffeur and eventually good friend, Ronald put on a new roof, put in a new kitchen, repainted the bedrooms, added a patio, dug out an old dried up pond they called "Lake Lucy". Ronnie and Barney also spent much of their time building the fence for the corral, cutting lumber, digging holes and sinking posts. The work was endless but for Ronnie, it was pure pleasure. He bought some cattle and a few horses. Once he had finished clearing the old trails, he would go horseback riding with Nancy and they would both enjoy their day, relishing the beauty and immensity of nature, breathing the clean fresh mountain air, and realizing that one of their most cherished dreams had come true.

Reagan's tenure as governor of California, from 1967 to 1975, was on the whole a successful one. His second term was certainly more fruitful and increased his popularity. He took important measures –even though some raised high controversy–. He vetoed bills to institute bilingual education or to decriminalize possession of small amounts of marijuana. To his liberal opponents' surprise, he signed one to legalize abortion – though Nancy was opposed to the practice – and opposed a state proposition that would have kept homosexual teachers away from public schools. He fought to preserve the quality of the California environment, creating anti-pollution agencies and helping to establish the Redwood National Park. In 1971, he worked with Bob Moretti, the Democratic Speaker of the Assembly, to pass the California Welfare Reform Act, the nation's first one of the kind, thus slowing the growth of welfare provisions that reduced undue benefits but increased funds for the "truly needy"—recipients of Aid for Families with Dependent Children. He took initiatives to reduce, though did not eliminate, state expenditure, especially in the fields of education and social services. He also froze the growth of the state workforce. He instituted programs to limit property taxes but also increased personal income taxes. Significantly, the annual state budget more than doubled during Reagan's two terms, rising from $4.6 billion in 1967 to $10.2 billion in 1974. It can be said that his eight-year record reflected his political talent as it marked a willingness to compromise while sticking to his conservative principles and deftly implementing most of his initial economic goals. And the recipe seemed to have paid as he was high in the polls when his second term came to an end.

Despite his popularity, he decided not to run for a third term. He preferred to swap his Sacramento office for simple down-to-earth activities such as cutting wood or going horseback riding on his ranch. He definitely needed some relief from the frenzy of public life.

Nancy's image after this long period had developed into an ambiguous even contradictory one.

She enjoyed the national limelight but feared the exposure from political success. She had given up the world of pictures for long now but the cameras and microphones had not vanished. The political sphere where she had been gravitating since her husband had occupied an elected office had made her life a fishbowl. A few bad experiences had made her more wary of the others, singling out carefully whom she could be talking to, whom she could trust, whom she could share her views with... Her life was a great deal more public and she equated the position with a form of alienation. She thought she was more vulnerable and had to be on the defensive most of the time. Through Ronnie, politics had given her some vicarious fame and power but it had also deprived her of protection and a sense of freedom.

Meanwhile, Nancy complemented her husband in a way that enhanced his charm but seemed occasionally to erode hers. His inexhaustible smile could frustrate or infuriate her, especially in case of conflict, be it for private or public matters. His passivity could arouse her passion. For example, his seemingly unfailing faith in his staff made her increasingly suspicious of them. She made a point of supervising his schedule and ordered changes when she deemed it necessary. She got very hard-nosed when things were not going exactly her way. Women were ordered to wear dresses. Men had to dress properly too. Lyn Nofziger, with his ugly and ridiculous Mickey Mouse tie, with his shirt constantly opened, had been the shame of the pack. The Reagan inner circle had to be 100% straight, vis-à-vis him, and vis-à-vis her. She could not tolerate adversity or the breaking of (her) rules. Her relationships with the press were imbued with fear, admittedly, but intimidation too. Some reporters had started to call her "the power behind the throne" as it seemed more and more clear to them that she exerted a strong behind-the-scene influence on her husband's decisions. Others, as did her stepdaughter a few years before, called her "the dragon lady".

If Nancy's public image reflected a complex, hard to make out yet already controversial personality, her private life also revealed a strong but overbearing character that generated incomprehension, disappointments, and tension.

Like Ronnie, she enjoyed the new ranch. But the rugged hideaway was more *his* territory than hers. He had long been desperately looking for such a vast open isolated land. Now he had it. "He loves it; she just, well, likes it", said a Reagan aide.[14] The house in Pacific Palisades, where they returned in January 1975, was hers. Still she saw her acceptance of the frequent stays up in the secluded Ynez Mountains as her gift to him, and she did not regret it as his joy reverberated on her. There could be no doubt about her infallible devotion to him. But the

---

[14] James A. Miller and Harry Benson, "Mrs. R's R&R", *Life*, October 1983, p. 4 8.

acquisition had not been her decision initially, it had been forced on her. The ranch was not *her* treasure. All proportions kept, the new property concealed a slight underlying frustration.

The most serious source of vexation as they started their post-Sacramento era was the children. Nancy loved them naturally but as always she was over-protective. She was very concerned about drugs and worried about how they could be immunized from the scourge spreading through schools and universities.

But at a time when all that most young people were looking forward to was autonomy, her motherliness seemed excessive. Patti and Ron felt stifled by her constant interference and sought refuge away from her.

Patti Reagan had changed her name into Patti Davis, surely not to mark her preference for her mom but as a distinct sign of independence from the Reagan label. She rebelled against her family name, rebelled against her parents' political stands, and rebelled against their lifestyle. After one year at Northwestern University, Illinois, where she developed her writing abilities, she returned to the West to study drama at the University of Southern California. Again, she stayed only one year. She could not care less about the value of a degree and a good career. Self-consciously unconventional, she became a groupie with one of the most popular rock groups of the time, the Eagles, and fell in love with guitarist and occasional banjo player Bernie Leadon. She started writing songs and the group recorded her "I Wish You Peace", which became a radio hit. Soon she was living with leather-clad Bernie, not even marrying, a decision that mortified her parents. Or Nancy, rather. Her father preferred to ignore the question. Like the press, Patti was mocking her mother's old-fashioned views on marriage. She shocked her mom as she let her know that love, not a wedding ring, was a prerequisite for sex. Nancy, whose own insecurity had always urged her to control everything, seemed to be losing ground in her power to manage family matters. She was losing her daughter and her inability to remedy the situation disoriented her. How could she have let her Patti get into a world that she had herself rejected as being bizarre, ugly, obscene, immoral? A world of long-haired, dangerous, anarchic young people who seemed systematically to oppose the rules of discipline, respect and propriety that she had been brought up with and had wanted to instill in her children. She both hated and feared the chaos they symbolized. But her powerlessness to communicate with her daughter gave rise to a sense of personal failure and made her feel guilty.

Ron, Jr., the Skipper, had been to the Webb School in Claremont, California. It was a strict all-boy boarding school that Nancy had selected to protect him from the sins and ravages of the counterculture. But soon he too would stray from the straight and narrow. He joined a group of unconventional friends who called themselves the "negos", young, so-called "negativist" boys who were constantly questioning the decisions of the administration. Ron developed a certain talent at discussing and arguing and became the leader of the defiant non-conformist group. They would slip out to parties at night or smoke marijuana in their dorm. Not even the dean, who had been prompted by Nancy, could get Ron to cut his long hair! Nancy was relieved when he eventually left the school and the group that had "corrupted" him. However he moved in with Mary Jane and Charles Wick during the last year in Sacramento.

Ron then joined Harvard where he discovered he had a passionate interest in the arts. But here again there was another unconventional group and the worried "mommy" would call again and again to check up on her son. It seemed that she would not let her son tread / get into an imperfect world. In other words she would simply not let him grow up. But the more she tried to hold him up, the more he slipped out of her hands. "Leave me alone! All I want is to be left alone!" he would yell furiously at his mother.[15] When her intrusions into his life became too unbearable, he would pack up and stay with friends or his sister for a week or two, or even longer.

Again the family Nancy had been so careful to protect seemed to be incomprehensibly torn apart. She had hoped to make her children grow up in her image but her efforts proved vain and seemed to give just the opposite results. Nancy was suffering and felt responsible for the disaster.

Ron soon gave his domineering but frustrated mother a new reason to worry. He decided to study dance with John West, a new teacher – the first black one – at Harvard. West had detected Ron's graceful body and enduring vitality and encouraged him to persevere in dancing. He had his four students work really hard to develop their intrinsic qualities. Ron, who embraced the discipline, wholeheartedly took an immense pleasure in it. Here was a new form of art through which he could exercise his creativity and refine his aestheticism. Dancing helped him flee from his busybody mother. Dancing meant freedom.

Nancy's source of trouble with her son lay less in dancing itself than in what it involved in terms of sexual identity. Compared to football players who projected the very image of virility and whose muscular bodies made girls on campus swoon, dancers had a reputation for being effeminate and, worst of all, gay. Nancy, for whom sexuality remained mostly taboo, all the more so when it came to her children, was getting increasingly worried and saw a new element in her life estrange her from her son.

---

[15] Leamer, op. cit., p. 241.

Was her private life inexorably deteriorating? She found strength in her faith in God and of course Ronnie was there, cheerful and optimistic as ever, convinced that better times would come. In addition, Ronnie's laidback attitude made the father and son relationship easier. In fact, the more distant Ron was from his mother, the closer he seemed to become to his father.

After leaving office, Ronald did not spend all his time in the ranch. Two of his former aides, Michael Deaver and Peter Hannaford, opened a public relations agency at 10960 Wilshire Boulevard in Westwood. They began booking the former governor a series of speaking engagements for which he received between $5,000 and $10,000 a speech. Reagan also voiced his political opinion in a daily three minute taped commentary to be used by more than 200 radio stations. The PR firm also worked it out with the Copley News Service to sell a weekly column written by Reagan to 174 newspapers. The various jobs kept him busy but still left him enough time to enjoy free days on the ranch. Not a bad combination for an income that, for the year 1975, was estimated at $800,000.

Ronald's money kept the family comfortable and his new mode of life filled him with pleasure. He traveled around, met people and could still deliver his political message. It was still basically the same simple conservative message, praising the virtues of capitalism and free enterprise, urging a return to moral principles and saving America and the world from the dangers of communism as incarnated by the Soviet Union. During these years he came out as one of the most prominent spokesmen for the conservative Republicans.

In May 1974, Ronald started meeting with a group of advisers at the Pacific Palisades house. The faithful circle of businessmen and political aides were there: Holmes Tuttle, Justin Dart, Ed Meese, Michael Deaver, Peter Hannaford, Lyn Nofziger – despite Nancy – James Lake and Washington attorney John Sears. After Nixon had resigned from office over the Watergate scandal – Reagan had defended him the whole way through – they worried about the way the most liberal wing was regaining control of the Republican party. Ronnie, who had flown in a rage when Gerald R. Ford had picked liberal Nelson Rockefeller for vice-president, had declined Ford's offer to be his secretary of transportation. He had been advised to do so in order to preserve his chance in case he should make up his mind to run for the upcoming 1976 election. As the group started discussing Ronnie's presidential prospects, they were wary about his running against an incumbent president. Ford himself tried to dissuade him from running. But sure of the role he had to play for his party and his country, growing more determined than ever, Ronnie decided he would take up the challenge of the Republican nomination, even against a sitting president.

Yet, after the 1968 setback, he had learnt an important lesson: contact his closest adviser and confidante, Nancy. Still the most protective wife, she was concerned about his health. Also, would he ruin his career if he lost? A whole lot of unanswerable questions arose but he found the right words to convince her of the validity of his mission. And there was no doubt in her mind that he was the right man to restore economic prosperity and moral leadership in America. Yes, she gave her blessing to Ronnie's bid for the presidency.

Nancy and her husband decided to invite their children for Halloween (1974) and tell them the big news themselves. Apart from Patti who would not see her parents at the time, they all came, Michael, Maureen and Ron. Their father explained that his candidacy was constantly solicited by his numerous supporters around the country. "It won't be easy, but the grassroots support is here. I've been speaking out on the issues for quite a while now, and it's time to put myself on the line. In three weeks, I'm going to announce that I'm entering the race. Otherwise, I'd feel like the guy who always sat on the bench and never got into the game."[16]

His campaign did not start in the best conditions. His former aide Stuart Spencer was now running Gerald Ford's campaign and Henry Salvatori, Taft Schreiber and Leonard Firestone, former good friends, now strongly rejected his candidacy as being party destructive, and joined the ranks of the Ford supporters. Nancy was furious at them for their flip-flop attitude and lack of loyalty. What irritated her most was the warmonger portrait Spencer had drawn of her husband in a series of scathing television commercials: "Remember, *Governor* Reagan couldn't start a war", the advertisements went, "but *President* Reagan could."

Nancy's public image during the primary campaign was made traditional, playing the quiet role of the deferential wife, traveling with Ronnie and casting her adoring gaze at him during his speeches. As ten years before, she held her standard question-and-answer sessions and interviews, had coffee talks with senior citizens, appeared at luncheons, always making sure to echo her husband's message: "I simply don't differ with Ronnie on anything significant. Surely we disagree on little things, but not on fundamental concepts," she insisted.[17] And indeed, she brought strong support to Ronnie's tough talk, unlike that of the moderate pro status quo Ford. The major points of Reagan's conservative platform included the need for a reinforced defense, a substantial budget cut, law-and-order and capital punishment. Yet he listened to Sears, his campaign director, who advised him to move his rhetoric slightly towards the center in order to reach the greatest number. As a result, Reagan's message turned out to be a subtle

---

[16] *My Turn*, op. cit., p. 181.
[17] "Political wives with different styles", *U.S. News & World Report*, March 8, 1976, p. 16.

compromise, mingling his own convictions with the desire to preserve the unity of his party and glean potential votes.

An unprecedented campaign fact appeared as the candidates' wives, Nancy and Betty Ford, paralleled their husbands' struggle by highlighting their distinct views on major questions.

However, they were women of the same generation. They had both attended New England prestigious schools, Smith (Nancy) and the Bennington School of Dance (Betty). They had both started artistic careers, Nancy as an actress and Betty as a dancer. The two had four children, even though Michael and Maureen Reagan were from Ronnie's first marriage, and both were appreciated for their good looks.

The primary election was marked by what was known as "the battle of the queens". As the campaign went along, Nancy and Betty seemed to have their own agendas, supporting their respective husbands. They both spoke out on the same issues, but with conflicting approaches. Betty advocated women's rights and strongly defended passage of the Equal Rights Amendment (ERA). Nancy was firm on traditional values and rejected the amendment proposed by feminists. She derided them as "just ridiculous", "silly women's libbers" and claimed that equality could not be reached through a constitutional change. "I really believe a woman's real happiness is found in the home with her husband and children. That doesn't mean they should not have interests, but they should be done in the framework of marriage, not in competition with marriage. That's where I think the women's libbers are in for trouble. God made men and women different, and they have different needs. . . . I think a woman gets more if she acts feminine."[18] She lambasted women who wore long pants as being "unfeminine" and criticized the then-new term "Ms" as it reflected a subversive culture of anti-marriage. Nancy's views mirrored her husband's most sincerely when it came to moral issues, denouncing vehemently the practice of abortion and the growing depravity in popular culture, particularly the rise of pornography and violence in "dirty" movies. Nancy was appalled when on August 10, 1975, Betty Ford told Morley Safer on "60 Minutes" that she would not be surprised if her daughter had sex before marriage or smoked marijuana. Mrs. Ford shared the view that pre-marital sex was a way to curb the divorce rate. She was 100% in favor of abortion and did not hide her satisfaction to see it legalized by the Supreme Court. Though the two women did not publicly rebuke each other, they did not hold each other in high esteem. At the end of a political dinner the Fords had hosted at their house in Palm Springs, Betty Ford laced into Nancy: "She's a cold fish", she told an aide.

---

[18] Kelley, op. cit., p. 193.

"Nancy could not have been colder. Then the flashbulbs went off, and she smiled and kissed me –suddenly an old friend. I couldn't get over that. Off camera –ice. On camera –warmth."[19] Nancy knew how to adapt her roles in front of cameras. Hollywood had taught her the lesson but, Betty thought, if the actress could be adorable, the real person inside was hypocritical and insincere.

Though he was unquestionably a great campaigner, haranguing the crowds with his natural oratorical gifts, Reagan lost the first five primaries and his campaign was $2 million in debt. Fortunately, because of the fund-raising efforts of his faithful aides bringing in extra contributions, the budget soon picked up. But close as the race was, at the Kansas City Convention in August 1976, Ford won the votes of 1,187 delegates to 1,070 for Reagan.

The battle was lost, certainly not the war. For the moment, what annoyed Nancy most was Mrs. Ford stealing the show at the convention. On the second night, as Nancy arrived on stage, the First Lady seized the moment to start dancing with singer Tony Orlando as the band played "Tie a Yellow Ribbon Round the Old Oak Tree". Mrs. Reagan, waving at the crowd, almost went unnoticed as all eyes were riveted upon Betty.

The next morning, the infallible supporters, Dart, Tuttle, Smith wanted to meet Reagan at his hotel room to exhort their favorite politician to accept the vice-presidency. As he came into the living-room to greet them, the telephone rang. "Right, right, right. Great. I'll do everything I can to help. Wonderful." He hung up and said to his friends: "Guys, I know what you came here for, but he's picked Bob Dole."[20]

Nancy took the blame for her husband's defeat as she was accused of acting behind the scenes and pushing him into running against Ford. Her role was emphasized, she was pointed to as the great orchestrator of the personnel's exits and entrances, new "Dragon Lady" stories appeared, depicting her as a "co-candidate", strong-willed and ambitious in her own right.

1976 was not Reagan's year. But it was not Gerald Ford's either as he was defeated by the Democrats' candidate, Jimmy Carter, in the general election.

Ronnie opposed just about any decision made by the Carter administration. Again, he gave hundreds of speeches denouncing the drift of his country, paralyzed as it was by what he called excessive taxes, "welfare cheats", unemployment and loss of sovereignty through counter-productive foreign policies such as the signing of the Panama treaty on April 18, 1978, an agreement he had as much anticipated as feared and attacked for years.

---

[19] *Ibid.*, p. 222; Leamer, op. cit., p. 251.
[20] Bob Colacello, "Ronnie and Nancy", *Vanity Fair*, July 1998, p. 140.

Soon a support committee was formed and as loyal Republicans kept joining in, it was turned into a Reagan for 80 team. Spirits were high as it appeared that eventually a million dollars were left from the previous campaign funds.

Now, would Ford run again in 1980? The answer was given by the former president himself when the Reagans once again were invited for a stay in Palm Springs at his retirement home. Not only would he not run but he would back Reagan's candidacy. Former tensions and resentments were forgotten. The hatchet was buried by the two men.

For Reagan now, the way was clear. Armed with a rich experience as a political leader, blessed with a great popularity around the nation, he could see the future positively. He would have four years to prepare for another run for the 1980 presidency. He had time to mobilize his troops and elaborate plans to occupy the pole position on the slate of Republican contenders.

But things did not come so easy.

In the early days of the campaign (1979), Nancy came to the fore as she became the mediator of personnel disputes. Tensions arose between John Sears, the brilliant 1976 campaign manager, a favorite of Nancy's, and Lyn Nofziger, whom she deemed profane and uncouth but in whom Ronnie saw a fine strategist. The two battled to get the control of the campaign. Nofziger was a poor fundraiser, Sears told Reagan. Nofziger said Sears was responsible for the 1976 debacle, which meant no good could be expected from a loser. But with Nancy's support, Sears was kept and on her insistence and to her great satisfaction, Nofziger was out, again. Then Sears feuded with Deaver, a good friend of Ronnie's. On Nancy's advice, though it tore her heart too, Ronnie reluctantly let Deaver out. Then Sears declared war against Edward Meese whom he accused of plotting to force him out of the campaign. It seemed that one quarrel spawned another quarrel and the whole campaign machine was having the hiccups.

The new front-runner in the Republican campaign was George Bush, a solid wealthy Texan who had had a successful career in oil business, had chaired the Republican National Committee, been Member of the U.S. House of Representatives, 1967-1971, U. S. ambassador to the United Nations, 1971-73, U.S. envoy to China, 1973-1974, and director of the CIA, 1976-1977.

It was decided and agreed upon that a Reagan-Bush debate should take place. Ronnie agreed to leave its organization and financing to a local newspaper, the *Nashua Telegraph,* though it intended to back Bush. But eventually they would not pay the expenses as it would be considered a corporate political contribution. They would just sponsor and moderate the debate. Ronnie knew that this confrontation would be a delicate one because the opponent was a clever politician and an expert on economics. John Sears, who realized that the Reagan

camp was paying for the event, decided the debate should not include just Reagan
and Bush but all the other candidates as well. Senator Howard Baker, Senator
Robert Dole, Congressman John Anderson, Congressman Philip Crane were
invited for the event at the high school in Nashua, New Hampshire. Reagan met
them and confirmed that he would not debate unless all the candidates could
participate. Politically, it sounded "fair play" and prevented Bush from appearing
as the strong guy. When they all arrived on the podium set up in the gymnasium,
Bush, who had just been informed of the others' presence, became indignant and
blamed Reagan for not respecting the rules that had been previously accepted by
the two camps. The crowd was obviously on Ronnie's side as it vociferously
called for a round-robin debate. But Bush, whose face now had turned stiff, his
features tense with anger, would not yield. Reagan, whose rate of adrenalin was
rising fast too, was no less flexible. The two looked undecided about what to do
and the situation seemed deadlocked. Suddenly, Jon Breen, editor of the *Nashua
Telegraph*, ordered the engineer to turn Ronnie's microphone off. The reply came
immediately. "I paid for this microphone, Mr. Green", retorted Ronnie, whose
indignation probably accounted for his mispronouncing the man's name. As a
matter of fact, he was right. He had paid for the whole expenses of the debate,
including the sound system. Eventually, Jim Lake, who knew the audience was all
for Ronnie, had a note sent to him on stage advising him to accept the one to one
debate. He complied and forgot about the other candidates. As each of the two
protagonists now developed his arguments, Bush seemed never to overcome his
anger and was truly a sorry sight. Reagan instead had the right tone at the right
moment, turning his anger into a renewed determination to convey the same
idealistic but patriotic message, just convincingly enough to electrify the
audience. His performance turned out a triumph.

And the test must have borne its fruit as Reagan defeated Bush by 27% in the
New Hampshire primary. Meanwhile, Nancy had asked Justin Dart to make a
report about the campaign's spending. It revealed such a huge deficit that on the
night of his victory, Reagan called Sears and his acolytes Jim Lake and Charles
Black, into his hotel suite in Manchester. Nancy was there too and acted as the
conciliator when Ronnie lost his temper. Yet the three men were kindly required
to sign their resignation. Sears was immediately replaced by William J. Casey, a
Wall Street banker and former chairman of the Securities and Exchange
Commission under Nixon. Once more, Mrs. Reagan seemed to have coordinated a
game of musical chairs. "Nancy had a lot to do with Sears's firing", said Frank
Donatelli, a regional campaign director. "She helped bring Casey aboard and was

very influential in the timing of the firing."[21] Ed Meese was appointed chief of staff for the campaign. Michael Deaver was reintroduced in the team and Nancy did not hide her satisfaction to see his services solicited again. So were Stuart Spencer's as it appeared that the campaign needed his clear-sightedness and political savvy. After he had joined the Ford team in 1976, Spencer had been on Nancy's black list. Yet it was Nancy in person who approached him and forgave his disloyalty. "Stu", she said, "I want you to know that bygones are bygones. . . . We need you."[22] Relieved by Mrs. Reagan's change of mind, he signed on to direct the campaign.

Ronnie eventually won the Republican nomination on the first ballot with 1,139 votes – George Bush received 37 – and took on Jimmy Carter, the incumbent president seeking a second term.

Nancy played a prominent role in the campaign. She was at Ronnie's side all the time, perfecting her smiling, well-groomed image, looking more gracious and caring than ever, nodding attentively and still gazing fondly at the husband-candidate. She gave her traditional question-and-answer sessions, and occasionally delivered a speech to fill in for Ronnie when his schedule was too heavy. But it was in his company that she felt clearly most comfortable and content, cheering him at countless rallies, luncheons and receptions. More importantly, her influence on the candidate was no longer subject to speculation. Her role indicated a greater involvement in the candidate's affairs than she admitted. In addition to giving Ronnie advice – to say the least – on the people he selected as aides, she constantly stimulated him and was his invigorator if he happened to be worn out or weary. Her presence boosted his confidence and observers commented extensively upon the better quality of his speeches when she was there. "She charges his batteries," said Jim Lake.[23] The campaign would have been nonsense without her. She had to be there. For the first time in the history of presidential campaigns, the race was led by a candidate and his wife through their love and mutual devotion. Their interdependence was their strength and alleviated the frequent blows the battle involved. As Mr. Reagan reminded in his autobiography: "When one of us has a problem, it automatically becomes a problem for the other; an attack on one of us is an attack on both of us. When one suffers, so does the other."[24] This was true as much in the public sphere as it was in private. The couple made no difference in their relationship. Nancy knew

---

[21] Leamer, op. cit., p. 269.

[22] Adler, op. cit., p. 157.

[23] *Look*, op. cit.

[24] Ronald Reagan, *An American Life: An Autobiography* (New York: Simon and Schuster, 1990), p. 167.

perfectly well how to read her husband's barometer. Time and again, she would need to calm down his Irish temper. Occasionally she would rescue him from the dangerous course in which his jovial and naïve style might embark him. Indeed his casual and offhand treatment of facts led him to make erroneous or inappropriate remarks. Once in 1979, as he was badgered by a reporter about pot smoking, he declared that marijuana smokers were twice as likely to develop lung cancer as smokers of regular cigarettes. As the dialogue progressed on to scientific details, and Nancy sensed that Ronnie was rambling on dangerous ground, she intervened strategically and unobtrusively, whispering in his ear: "Tell him you wouldn't know".

"I wouldn't know," he exclaimed, too happy to cut that conversation short as he eventually realized a trap had been set for him.[25]

Nancy also helped her favorite candidate by slightly moderating her own position on sensitive questions, in particular as regards women's issues. The press corps, in particular young females, criticized her for her unwillingness to address those issues. She did speak about them but watered down her speech, making sure the impact would not affect Ronnie's overall positive image. Contrary to 1976, though she still rejected abortion and the passage of the ERA, she now advocated equal pay for equal rights. Did such a view reflect a significant evolution in her approach to women's rights? Most observers doubted it and interpreted it as a political stratagem to counterbalance Ronnie's occasional hard line conservative speech. But, like Ronnie, she remained convinced that the time for liberal politics in a permissive society had passed and her moderation on minor points did not contradict her firm conservative stance. It simply highlighted her sharp political instincts. Her interviews were peppered by soft but non-controversial phrases such as "honesty", "integrity", "peace", "freedom", "the American way of life", "getting back to the basics"…

What she tried to do, probably more than anything, was to differentiate herself from Rosalynn Carter who publicly confessed her influence. "The President of the United States cares what I think," the First Lady said in a 1979 speech. "I find myself in the eye of history. I have influence. And I know it."[26] Nancy positioned herself as the exact opposite of Mrs. Carter. "I am not the driving, pushing force behind him," she insisted. "I support my husband, of

---

[25] Leighton, op. cit., p. 165.

[26] Jill Gerston, « Rosalynn Carter sticks to the task at hand », *The Philadelphia Inquirer*, 14 October 1980, p. 1D.

course, but I am not a driving force."[27] She also told the press that it was not proper for First Ladies to sit in on Cabinet meetings, as Mrs. Carter did.

As the campaign went on, Reagan took an immense delight in lampooning Jimmy Carter just as wittily as he had mocked Governor Pat Brown in California. He had no equals in this game of sarcasms and he knew that his humor made his charm and won the crowds over to him. A good series of one-liners could be more effective than a brilliant but soporific speech on the future of the economy.

After Reagan had blamed Carter for getting the country into a depression, the sitting president had shot back lecturing the former Hollywood actor with the expert terminology of a university professor: "That shows how little he knows. This is a recession." Reagan was not long to reply: "If the President wants a definition, I'll give him one. Depression is when you're out of work," he said. "A recession is when your neighbor's out of work. Recovery is when Carter's out of work." Cheers.

In Detroit, he almost adopted Martin Luther King's tone, but the effect was totally different : "I had a dream the other night. I dreamed that Jimmy Carter came to me and asked me why I wanted his job. I told him I didn't want *his* job. I wanted to be President."[28]

Nancy remained attentive all the while and tried to keep her sound acumen to analyze the situation objectively and prevent her husband from making an embarrassing public blunder. As the campaign was drawing to a close, the major obstacle to overcome was the debate between the two candidates. In the age of the almighty media, the confrontation, now a tradition, had to be prepared meticulously. An inopportune statement and the whole campaign efforts could be instantly annihilated. There are always a number of undecided volatile voters who, at the last minute, can swing their votes for the opponent. As the polls revealed no candidate had significant lead, the upcoming debate was taken extremely seriously by both camps.

Despite his advantage as being the current occupant of the White House, Carter had a terrible burden on his back. He was tangled up in what was known as "the Iran crisis" where sixty-six Americans had been seized by Islamic student militants and held hostage for a year. The repetitive effect of press reports on and television images of blindfolded U.S. citizens detained in the heavily guarded U. S. embassy in Tehran moved and angered the American nation. To make it worse, in May Carter had approved a supersecret operation by American military commandos to rescue the hostages. Unfortunately, the helicopters involved

---

[27] Jill Gerston, « The Stargazer : She has both eyes on Reagan –and his campaign. » *The Philadelphia Inquirer*, 13 October 1980, p. 1D.

[28] Adler, op. cit., p. 160 and Leighton, op. cit., pp. 164-165.

suffered from serious mechanical problems. One crashed into a transport aircraft in a remote desert, killing eight soldiers. Jubilant Iranians then dispersed the hostages to various hideouts across their country making any other rescue operation impossible. The accident and the human losses came as a humiliating blow to the superpower and the whole mismanagement of the crisis appeared to the world as a conspicuous military, diplomatic and political fiasco. Naturally it was Carter who took the blame for that "desert debacle" and in spite of his genuine efforts to free his fellow citizens – he managed to conclude an agreement that would eventually lead to the release of the hostages – he had great difficulty not to appear weak and ineffective. Republicans put the blame on Carter and took advantage of the situation.

The debate took place in Cleveland on October 28, 1980. On stage the two candidates now played their last cards. They started presenting their programs with their most persuasive arguments and eloquence. The real battle came as Jimmy Carter attacked Ronald Reagan by depicting him as an advocate of nuclear proliferation and a bomb-happy warmonger. Though the issue did have its importance, Mr. Carter ridiculed himself when he confessed he had discussed the question with his daughter Amy. By consulting a little schoolgirl on the use of nuclear arms, he was giving the country a poor image of himself, both as a father and as a president. And it was Reagan who, paradoxically but unequivocally, appeared as Mr. Peace.

Carter, off balance and growing tense, then lashed at Reagan on Medicare, arguing that since his days as Governor of California, he had always sided with the rich, to the detriment of the poor, systematically criticizing Social Security and health care.

"There you go again," came Ronnie's famous reply with a self-confident smile. He went on with the right persuasive words of "the great communicator" he was now known to be. And, with the same grave solemn tone a president uses on historic moments, he addressed the nation: "Are you better off than you were four years ago? Is it easier for you to go out and buy things in the stores than it was four years ago? Is there more or less unemployment in the country than there were four years ago? Is America respected throughout the world as it was? Do you feel that our security is as safe, that we're as strong as we were four years ago?

If you answer all of those questions yes, why then I think your choice is very obvious as to who you'll vote for. If you don't agree, if you don't think that this course that we've been on for the last four years is what you would like to see us follow for the next four, then I could suggest another course that you have.

"I would like to have a crusade today, and I would like to lead that crusade.... one to take government off the backs of the great people of this country, and turn you loose again to do those things that I know you can do as well, because you did them and made this country great."[29]

After the debate, the press commented widely on Carter's somber look and poor eloquence. His undeniable expertise on economic and social problems had no impact. His mastery of figures and details was overcome by his failure to charm and convince. On the contrary, Ronnie's performance was a smashing triumph. As often during the campaign, there had been no mark of genius in his speech but he had artfully displayed his speaking talents. Despite his approximate knowledge of issues, despite his failure to present miraculous solutions, despite his age, 69, he aroused popular enthusiasm with his good looks, magnetic charm and charisma and was propelled as the political leader the country needed to restore confidence and power. One week later, on Election Day, the advantage acquired from the debate was materialized into victory as Reagan discomfited his Democratic opponent by receiving 43,899,248 votes, that is 50.75%, leaving Carter far behind with 35,481,435 votes, or 41,02%. Reagan obtained 489 electoral college votes against 49 for Carter. The incumbent president carried only six states.

The victory was Ronnie's but Nancy was definitely close at hand. Years later, their son Ron confessed about his mother's involvement in Ronald's affairs: "I think if left to his own devices, he might have ended up hosting *Unsolved Mysteries* on TV," he said, emphasizing the fact that his mother was the key to his father's ascension to the White House.[30]

Yes indeed the Reagan political career had been a team affair. And most importantly, there was a woman behind the throne. James Rosebush, who would later become Nancy's Chief of Staff at the White House, even quantified Nancy's role: "The political strategy which brought him to the White House was 50% his own, 25% from his friends and advisors, and 25% from Nancy Reagan."[31] Such assessment is quite questionable for it seems difficult to measure with scientific precision the political influence the candidate's wife played in the victory. How is it possible to claim that a man can reach the White House without mastering his success? It seems reasonable to affirm that he is fully responsible for his career, whatever the support he receives from his advisors, consultants and advocates. Reagan's decisions, his power of conviction and his undeniable magnetism were not artifices created by professional handlers. And similarly, what does a quarter of his success cover exactly? What is the strategic portion Nancy represented? Did the 25% limit her to a "decorative" role or did it reflect a deeper political

---

[29] Leamer, op. cit., p. 281.
[30] *U. S. News & World Report*, October 18, 1999, p. 14.
[31] James Rosebush, *First Lady, Public Wife* (Lanham, MD : Madison Books, 1987), p. 110.

involvement? In either case, what was the real effect of her action? The whole process of victory is hard to analyze as there are myriad more or less identifiable factors that can influence the final result.

Yet, despite the quantification inaccuracy, all the analysts' comments concur to signal Nancy's role as a major one. She had no political ambition of her own. Her only ambition had been to ensure his success. And for this purpose, she had displayed a total devotion to his presidential goals. But through love, the devotion had not been – was not – one-sided: it had operated both ways and emerged as a partnership. For Nancy, the support and help she brought to her husband was part of her obsessive desire to be a perfect wife.

The concept of the First Couple had appeared in the first part of the twentieth century, with Franklin and Eleanor Roosevelt. But each Presidency brought its own specific tandem in the White House. The Roosevelts had respect for each other but no love. The Trumans and Eisenhowers had love but Bess and Mamie played no political part. The "Jack and Jackie" image had been created for the media. Mrs. Kennedy pleased her husband by being glamorous but remained politically self-effacing. Betty and Gerald Ford did not stay long enough to reveal the whole dynamics of their partnership. Rosalynn Carter had been too powerful and somewhat belittled her husband. How would the Reagan couple evolve with the Presidency?

For the moment, the tandem relished "their" success, in public and in private. But what they needed most was a good rest at Rancho Del Cielo just to be together breathing the fresh air of the Santa Ynez Mountains. Three years before, on their twenty-fifth wedding anniversary, Ronnie had offered Nancy a wonderful gift. He had never forgotten what she had once told him about her romantic idea of a marriage proposal. The boy would take the girl out in a canoe and play the ukulele while she would drag her hand in the water. Eager to make her dream come true, he had taken Nancy out to Lake Lucky, their little pond. He had led her by the hand to the waterside where a nice little canoe had been tied to the shore. It had been symbolically named "Truluv".

"I don't have a ukulele," he had said in his most sentimental voice, "but I have a harmonica."

"That'll do," she had replied with that indescribable delight of a woman whose constant quest for perfection had been rewarded by this love boat. They had embarked and paddled gently across the little expanse of water. He had played one or two harmonica tunes. She had had it all. The romantic serenade in a love boat...

Both "Mommie" and "Daddy" craved for another such perfect romantic break before the hoopla of inauguration celebration and the ensuing pressure of presidential responsibilities.

Only then would they find the strength to face the new challenges ahead...

Part IV

FIRST LADY:
THE FIRST YEAR, THE WORST YEAR

Just a few weeks after the election, Ron called his parents:

"Mom, I'm getting married."
"When?"
"Tomorrow. We want it real simple."

On 24 November 1980, as the rain was falling in sheets on New York, Ronald Prescott Reagan, the Skipper, and Doria Palmieri, whom he had met at Stanley Holden, the ballet company, were declared man and wife. The daughter of an Italian immigrant, born in Genoa, who worked as a set designer for 20th Century Fox and an all-American mother, Doria was a pretty dark-eyed, curly-haired, little brunette whom Ron said looked like singer Linda Ronstadt. She had joined him in New York when he had won his dance scholarship to the Joffrey II Ballet the year before. Nancy was slightly upset that she would not attend her son's wedding. She had certainly dreamed of a grander and more dignified celebration: How come she could not give her son away, with a fine solemn marriage ceremony? She could have arranged a big wedding party and invited her favorite friends. Her frustration was exacerbated by the fact that Ron was marrying a girl seven years older than him. This was not the ideal match she had figured out!

But everything was not so bad. Nancy was glad that her son had married a girl who did accept to give up her own dancing career to make her husband's easier. That is the stuff love is made of, she thought. Also, both Reagan parents enjoyed the idea that marriage erased all suggestion that their son could be a homosexual.

Silly as it might be, the public perception of a boy pursuing a dancing career was still that of an effeminate. The virile image was now restored. And the whole family image was more appropriate. So much the better for the political image of the president-elect.

The Inauguration event approaching, tension grew in the Reagan clan as the media scrutiny became everyday more important. It was the transition from Rosalynn to Nancy that caused the first post-election controversy. As goes the tradition, the current First Lady gave the new arrival a tour of the Executive Mansion. The result was Nancy was dismayed by Rosalynn's lack of taste in décor. The presidential mansion was not worthy of its name and welcome function. How could she greet foreign dignitaries in such a drab and uninviting setting? She estimated that a lot of redecoration work was absolutely necessary... and urgent! So much so that a rumor was circulating that she had asked the Carters to move out of the White House a few days early in order to start the redecoration, leaving Rosalynn shocked and deeply hurt. Television specials and editorials exploited and magnified the incident, causing great turmoil even within the Republican Party, some of whose members openly denounced Mrs. Reagan's paradoxical lack of propriety. Of course Nancy denied trying to enter the White House before the due date and explained that all she wanted was to facilitate the job of the White House staff by spreading their removal work over several days instead of a few hours.

A series of nicknames appeared or reappeared in the negative press such as "The Iron Orange", "The Evita of Santa Barbara", "Mommy Dearest", "The Dragon Lady", "Little Gun", the latter referring to Mrs. Reagan's firings of staff and the "tiny little handgun" she once said she kept at her bedside when Ronnie was off on travel.

Nancy felt shocked and angry too but she suppressed her negative feelings and focused on the Inaugural. In the days preceding the big event, National Airport offered a dazzling parade of corporate and private jets, all belonging to the Reagans' long guest list of millionaire friends and celebrities from the business, entertainment and political world. Washington D.C. became the center of the world and the scene of splashy cocktail receptions, candlelit dinners, elegant balls and galas, fireworks and laser shows, all specially organized to entertain this attractive beau monde. The Reagans were invited to many private parties but understandably attended few. One of the most sought-after invitations was a dinner dance given by Nancy and Wyatt Dickerson for the Armand Deutsches at "Merrywood", their estate in McLean, Virginia. The Reagans attended the elegant event at the childhood home of Jacqueline Bouvier.

Unlike the Carters who had planned a very "cheap" common man's Inaugural in 1977, the Reagans made things big. There were eight white-tie Inaugural balls, at $100 a ticket, for standing room only, and $2,000 to sit down. These counted among the more reasonably priced events. Free festivities, as those of the Carter Inauguration, had disappeared. The total cost of the Reagan Inauguration amounted to $16 million, the most lavish and expensive in American history.

The swearing-in ceremony took place on January 20, 1981. For the first time in American presidential history, it was held on the terrace of the Capitol's west front, which offered a magnificent view down the Mall to the Washington Monument. Previous Inaugurations had been held on the east portico, which looked out on a parking lot. At the Inaugural stand, the first row was occupied by the Reagan family and the Bushes and the former administration, the Carters and the Mondales. But they were all here. The children: Patti, Ron and his new wife Doria; Maureen and Michael, Ronnie's children from his first marriage, and their respective spouses Dennis Revell and Colleen Sterns; Dr. Loyal and Edith of course; Richard, Nancy's stepbrother and his wife Patricia; Cousin Charlotte and her husband Jim Ramage; Moon, Ronald's brother Neil and his wife Bess. And naturally Nancy's friends of The Group were present with their husbands, with the Bloomingdales at their head. Jerry Zipkin, Frank Sinatra, "Ole Blue Eyes", Estée Lauder, Bob Hope, Jimmy Stewart, . . . The list was impressive: stars from showbiz, artists, athletes, successful publishers, prominent industrialists, political friends, diplomats and international connections.

Now came the historic and emotional moment. The whole assembly kept standing in absolute silence as if holding their breath while the former broadcaster, screen actor, and Governor of California Ronald Reagan started taking his oath of office, with his hand on his mother's bible. Chief Justice Warren Burger administered the ceremony. Nancy's eyes were wet but her face was illuminated with a triumphant smile.

As Ronald said the words, "I, Ronald Wilson Reagan, do solemnly swear, ..." radio and television programs were giving the great news: "After 444 days, the hostages have just been released, ...", sounding like the thrilling climax of the Iran hostage crisis. Carter had worked up to the last moment to secure the release of the last 52 hostages, but Iranian leader Ayatollah Khomeini waited until Reagan was sworn in before allowing the plane to take off. This was a dramatic moment indeed, just like a perfect movie.

Then with great solemnity, Ronald delivered his Inaugural address. Like John F. Kennedy a few decades before, he wore a formal morning attire including a gray club jacket, a gray vest and gray striped pants. Behind him, Nancy wore a $3,000 red coat and dress by Adolfo, with a bright oval hat to match, not unlike

Jackie Kennedy's famous pillbox hat. She also carried a tiny $1,650 alligator purse by Judity Leiber.

The whole Inaugural celebration took place in a warm and joyful atmosphere of elegance and good taste. True, some guests complained about the excessive prices but still, the organization was unanimously deemed first-class.

Yet, despite the favorable comments of most participants, and the very positive interest and support of the Washingtonian population, Nancy's new set of difficulties began with the Inauguration. It was her extravagant wardrobe that brought things to a head. Her ensemble included a gown valued at $25,000, a $10,000 mink coat, a $1,700 dress and a fur-lined raincoat. Her one-shoulder white beaded sheath dress for the Inaugural Tuesday night ball had been designed by James Galanos. Cost: $10,000; she wore custom-made dancing slippers by David Evins. Cost: $200; and also sported a white satin evening bag by Leiber. Cost: $400. Elegance has its price but it seems that once more the initial public enthusiasm going along with the festive atmosphere had a sour aftertaste. The First Lady's flashy style and social flair that had drawn admiration were now assailed by a barrage of blistering criticism in the local and national press.

There was also widespread rumor that again she was wielding tremendous power and influence behind the scenes, especially by overseeing the appointments of the president's Cabinet and vetoing some of the selections.

Two and a half weeks after they changed their address from Pacific Palisades to 1600 Pennsylvania Avenue, on February 6, the new president turned seventy. In no way would Nancy let the first birthday celebration as president remain an insignificant affair. In secret, she planned a surprise party in honor of her husband. No detail was left to chance.

Her hair was usually done by Robin Weir but for special occasions like this one, Julius Bengtsson, her California hairdresser, would come all the way from Los Angeles. Mrs. Reagan also wanted her nails done by Jessica Vartoughian, the L. A. nail maven whose star-studded clientele included such ringing names as Joanna Carson, Linda Gray, Raquel Welch and Barbra Streisand. Nancy paid for Jessica's flight from Los Angeles to Washington to prepare her nails for the big occasion.

She planned a rather intimate dinner at Jean Louis, a fashionable restaurant at the Watergate, with surprise guests like Jimmy Stewart and his wife Gloria, Ted Graber, the L.A. interior designer, members of the Group, former aides like Henry Salvatori or members of his Cabinet such as the new Attorney General William French Smith. The cost of a dinner for two: about $250. But this dinner was just a sham. The birthday highlight was the surprise party she planned at the White House for the next day, this time with a hundred guests, the list being largely dominated by Californians. Maureen was the only child who could attend that day. Nancy had carefully kept the event secret and told Ronnie that the dinner at Jean-Louis had been the real party. A small group of additional friends would come to the White House for a light birthday dinner.

Ronnie became somewhat suspicious when, getting ready for the "casual" dinner, he heard some bustle downstairs:

"It certainly sounds like more than twenty people down there", he said with a frown.

Nancy cleared her throat. "Well, you know how all that marble makes the noise reverberate," she replied innocently.

A few minutes later, they joined their guests. Nancy opened the door to the State Dining Room.

"You fooled me," Ronnie exclaimed, as the "crowd" started singing "Happy birthday to you, Mr. President".

Once again, they had a sumptuous evening. Nancy was radiant with her swept-back chignon, diamond and pearl drop earrings and her long white-beaded gown. The decoration was gorgeous: flowers everywhere to make the room a spring garden; the food was excellent, including lobster and veal; they laughed and had fun; they danced between each course.

Cameras did not miss Nancy and Frank Sinatra dancing on "Nancy With the Smiling Face". But soon Ronnie was cutting in for another dance and after a few steps another man was cutting in and another man again. Maureen reserved one dance for her father. Once more, Nancy was praised for her unique savoir-faire as a hostess. Chefs in white coats and hats brought a huge birthday cake to every table. Each was topped with a symbolical white horse. Ronald was its rider, the new American hero.

They danced until late in the night. Everyone had a great time.

Some time later, Ron was making his debut with the Joffrey II at the Metropolitan Opera House in New York City. Ronnie and Nancy attended a gala benefit to see their son perform in the ballet, *Unfolding*, in which he appeared with Melissa Zamoia. The ballet, choreographed by Gray Veredon, a New Zealand dancer, was abstract and hard to understand as a whole but its beauty did not escape the Reagan parents who, from their box, did not miss a second of their son's graceful motion on the big stage Nancy was jubilant and after the performance, in a private room backstage, she congratulated her son and gave him a big hug. "I'm so proud of you!" she told him as they rubbed noses together.

It was the last Sunday in March 1981. Spring was showing its early signs, the sun's rays barely warming the chilly air and resting their gentle light on the cherry blossoms of Pennsylvania Avenue. The president and his wife decided to walk to

St. John's Episcopal Church on Lafayette Square. On their way they talked about the week to come. Ronnie referred to an important vote by the Senate on his bill to cut $41 billion from the proposed Carter budget. If it passed, it would mean that for the first time since 1933 when Franklin D. Roosevelt took office, government spending would decline and the economy could pick up. If it failed, then Ronnie would be in great trouble. But Ronnie was an eternal optimist. The following day, March 30th, saw the weather take a more dreary turn. The sky was overcast and moist with continuous drizzle. It was the president's seventieth day in office. His hundred days would be over soon, a date when the first assessments are made and compared with other presidents. Like every morning now, he met with the White House troïka of top aides: Chief of Staff James Baker, Presidential Counselor Edwin Meese, and Deputy Chief of Staff Michael Deaver. Then he delivered a speech to 140 subcabinet-level employees. After lunch, he had a nap in his bedroom before he addressed 3,500 members of the AFL-CIO at the Hilton Hotel at 2:00.

Nancy could not be present for the speech. Her day was very busy too as she attended a midmorning philanthropic reception at the Phillips Gallery of Art with Barbara Bush, the wife of the vice president, Peter McCoy, her chief of staff and Muffie Brandon, her social secretary. Soon afterward, they were driven to Georgetown to lunch with some Cabinet wives at the "Q" Street house of Michael Ainslie, president of the National Trust for Historic Preservation. For some reason, Nancy was feeling a little nervous and though she enjoyed the luncheon, she was anxious to leave early. She excused herself and was driven back to the White House. Hardly had she been meeting in the third-floor solarium with Ted Graber and Rex Scouten when George Opfer, the head of her Secret Service detail, told her there had been a shooting at the Hilton but the president was all right: "Some people were wounded, but your husband wasn't hit. Everybody's at the hospital." The news had the effect of an electric shock through her whole body. There was no time to lose. She demanded to be driven to George Washington Hospital immediately. There is no word to express how guilty she felt not to have been with him at this particular moment when he needed her more than ever. For so many years, she had been his constant protector. The feeling was unbearable. The drive seemed endless as the street was jammed with police cars and radio and TV reporters swarming to the scene. As she rushed from the limousine through the double doors of the emergency room, she yelled "He's all right, he's all right!" to the horde of photographers and reporters. She was met by Mike Deaver who had the unpleasant task of telling her what she had feared most:

"He's been hit," he said.

"But they told me he *wasn't* hit," she answered as if refusing to accept the truth.

"Well, he was. But they say it's not serious."

"*Where? Where* was he hit?" she asked.

"They don't know. They're looking for the bullet."

The word "bullet" scared her and resonated in her head like a detonation.

"I've got to see him!" she said instinctively.

"You can't. Not yet."

"Wait a minute. If it's not serious, *why can't I see him?*"

She was ushered into a tiny office that for the occasion served as a waiting-room. As she insisted on seeing her husband, Deaver went off to find out when she could. The whole scene was a nightmare. Jim Brady, Ronnie's press secretary, had been seriously wounded in the head and the prognosis left him little chance of survival. Timothy McCarthy, a Secret Service agent, had also been shot. Officer Thomas K. Delahanty had been taken to another hospital. Nurses kept coming in and giving ever more alarming news. Doctors first thought that Ronnie had had a heart attack. Then Nancy was told they could not find his pulse and he might go into a shock treatment. Then they said his left lung had been hit. But she still did not know the true facts of what increasingly appeared to be a tragedy.

She learned the whole truth much later...

After his speech, the president had walked briskly out of the Hilton, turned, smiled and waved to the gathered crowd. Then came the shooting. It all happened so fast. As the first shot rang out, Secret Service agent Jerry Parr shoved the president facedown onto the floor of his limousine and yelled "Take off! Take off!" to the driver.

"You son-of-a-bitch!" Ronnie told Parr as the car screeched off at high speed, "You broke my ribs." He could hardly breathe as Parr lay over him as a shield of protection. The Secret Agent ordered the driver to go to the White House. When he saw the president was coughing up blood, he understood that George Washington University was the more appropriate destination. "Rawhide not hurt," he radioed to an agent in the car behind, using the president's code name. He was of course lying to mislead listeners of the Secret Service frequency, and hoping that his colleague would get the message that President Reagan was unfortunately badly hurt. Ronnie did not know he had been shot. "I feel like I can't breathe," he said as he got out of the car. His knees began to buckle and he was carried by two agents, a paramedic and a nurse into the emergency room. The room was so packed with policemen, Secret Service men, White House aides and doctors all talking at the same time that Wendy Koenig could not hear his heart through the stethoscope. Two nurses tore and cut off his clothes and when a doctor lifted his left arm, they found the bullet hole.

They eventually located a .22 bullet. Just a quarter of an inch from the heart! The president had been hit by a so-called "Devastator" bullet, designed to explode on contact. Luckily this one had not. After ricocheting off the presidential armored limo, it had flattened out into the size of a dime and pierced Reagan under his arm. Doctors' later diagnosis was that it had bounced into his seventh rib and veered off into the left lower lobe of his lung. He had lost so much blood – five pints!

A twenty-five-year-old blond man, John Hinckley, Jr., from Evergreen, Colorado, was responsible for that shooting. He had fired six bullets at nearly point-blank range in less than two seconds before being wrestled to the ground. Had Tim McCarthy not thrust himself before him, the president would have been killed. The young man would later confess that he wanted to assassinate the president to impress actress Jodie Foster. He believed that by doing so, he and Foster would be forever united in heaven.

Nancy was horrified when she was eventually admitted into her husband's room. The place was strewn with torn clothes, plastic bags, scissors, tubes, bandages and blood stains. Ronnie was lying on his narrow bed with an oxygen mask on his ashen face and bottles hanging over him. His lips were caked with blood. She leaned over to kiss him.

"Honey, I forgot to duck," he said with an almost inaudible voice behind his mask. Even under such tragic circumstances, he had kept his sense of humor.

Forty-eight-year-old Dr. Benjamin Aaron, the head of the Cardiothoracic Surgery at GW decided that the president had to be operated on because blood continued to flow from his chest into the tube. It was a delicate but necessary step to take.

"If we don't operate, we might get into some problems," Aaron told Nancy. "The operation's the surest, the safest path at the time."

Nancy gave her accord. They spared her the legal but superfluous written statement and accepted a verbal consent. As Ronnie was wheeled down the halls to OR 2, the largest operating room, Nancy's heart began to pound uncontrollably and her eyes grew wet. She held his hand all the way fighting her tears away. As she let the long procession of doctors and nurses shuttle the presidential bed into surgery, another bed was taking a similar direction. It was press secretary Jim Brady who, with his skull shattered, was hardly recognizable.

Inside OR 2, Ronnie made an effort to raise his head and pronounce a few words before the operation.

"I hope you people are all Republicans," he said looking up at the doctors.

"Today, we are *all* Republicans, Mr. President," answered Dr. Joseph Giordano, who in reality was a liberal democrat.

A few hours later, Nancy was admitted into the recovery room and could hardly stand the view of her husband attached to those scary machines, an EKG monitor and a respirator. He was rigged out with two chest tubes for drainage, another into his mouth for breathing, his whole body was covered with lines and pulse monitors and IVs. His face was pale gray and had lost all its natural energy and radiance.

"I love you," she said and burst into tears. She grabbed his arm and they looked at each other quietly for a while. The people present were moved by the First Couple's love scene. One of the doctors later described it as a "genuine and absolutely pure display of love, amazing, incredibly touching, overpowering."[1]

He could not speak with the tube in his mouth and could not breathe either. When he saw the clipboard that they had put at his side for him to communicate, he wrote a note on it: "I can't breathe."

Nancy's worries increased. Was the suffocation serious? She turned to the doctors and as her husband's infallible protector, acted as his interpreter. "He can't breathe", she said emphatically.

"You shouldn't worry, Mrs. Reagan," answered Dr. Edelstein. "You see the machine is doing the breathing for him. He's having difficulty because he isn't used to it yet."

She insisted: "He says he can't breathe."

Then Ron, Jr., was in the room at his father's bedside. On hearing the news of the shooting, he had taken the first plane all the way from Lincoln, Nebraska, where he was performing with Joffrey II. "Dad, it's all right," he whispered in his father's ear. He explained he had had the same choking sensation when he first went scuba diving because of the mask. His presence was a great source of comfort for Ronnie. Their relationship had suffered some kind of strain over the years but crucial moments like this one demonstrated that their love was intact.

When doctors asked Nancy to leave the room, she just did not want to, repeating that she had to be at his side because he needed her. Gently but firmly, Dr. Edelstein prompted her outside. As she walked out, she kept looking at him and could guess what he had in his mind. He could not breathe.

Back in the White House, Nancy was feeling terribly insecure, demoralized, despondent. The trauma kept her lonely and crying long hours. She did not get an hour's sleep in the three days following the attempted assassination. She lost her

---

[1] Laurence Leamer, *Make-Believe: The Story of Nancy & Ronald Reagan* (New York: Harper and Row, 1983), p. 318.

appetite. All she could do was look out her window and think about her husband, his courage, his pain, his narrow escape, his constant humor throughout his ordeal. But most of her time was spent at the hospital. She had to be there to take care of him and make sure that he did not miss anything or his state was not aggravating. She brought him a photograph of the two of them and said: "I don't want you to forget what I look like."

Now Ronnie was fully conscious and though his chest still hurt, he knew he was going to recover. His witty nature took the upper hand as he entertained the nurses with his jokes again, which was also a way to forget his pain. As he had trouble breathing, he scrawled a note:

"Send me to Los Angeles where I can see the air I'm breathing".

The message made everyone laugh. Then he wrote another one:

"If I'd had this much attention in Hollywood, I'd have stayed there."

The whole medical team were delighted to have such a prestigious yet cheerful patient. It was so pleasant to see a man – not an anonymous man! – who had endured a very serious operation and was covered with surgical tubes demonstrate such a lesson of courage. In the same situation, most patients look sad or demoralized. Ronnie was funny!

"I have to be. My father-in-law is a doctor," the president wrote.

But some of his notes showed that his humor was like a veil that concealed some deep anxiety:

"Will I be able to ride my horses again? Will I be able to cut brush?"

Then he worried about his staff:

"Was anyone else hurt?" he asked.

It was Dan Ruge, the White House physician, who told him what had happened. Nancy was there too. She apprehended his reaction when he heard about the three other wounded men.

"Damn!" he murmured as tears welled up in his eyes.

"Was Jim hit in the head?"

Nancy nodded and he repeated "Damn! Damn!" knocking on his bed, feeling so sorry for his press secretary who, doctors said, would not die but might be permanently paralyzed.

"He was very upset that other people were hurt just because of their involvement with him," Dr. Paul Colombani said.[2]

All the children came to visit their father: Patti, Maureen, Michael and his wife Colleen. They were a great comfort to Ronnie. He received flowers, candies and all sorts of "get well" messages from the four corners of the country. Soon

---

[2] *Ibid.*, p. 321.

staffers came to his room to have him sign papers. Nancy noted that it had taken Lyndon Johnson four weeks after his gall bladder operation to resume work! Though it was not "business as usual" yet, Ronnie's condition was making great progress. The hospital spokesperson declared to the press that the president was now low on medication and he was doing extremely well. He walked a little bit now.

But Nancy knew more about her husband than what press releases announced. She had a new source of worry tormenting her mind. Ronnie had lost his appetite and began to run quite a high temperature, hovering between 102 and 103 degrees. He began to look pale and glum and lethargic. Fortunately a bronchoscopy revealed he had developed no infection around the wounded area in his chest. But doctors could not diagnose what was wrong. Nancy knew that he would not recover until he started eating again. She had the White House chef, Anne Allman, prepare his favorite split-pea soup, hamburger soup, turkey soup. But he would not touch a thing. Some friends from the West coast flew to Washington and brought containers of "Reagan-special" soup. To no avail.

One evening, Nancy arrived at the hospital all dressed up telling him they were going out for dinner.

"I found a little disco on the way to the hospital," she said.

"Oh, great," he grumbled, not very convinced yet ready to accept the offer.

"Are you going to come along with me?"

He made an effort to get out of his bed and started to get dressed.

"Not necessary," she said with a smile and she led him into a room where she had set up two chairs and a table with two trays full of food in front of a television set. He asked about what was on tonight.

"It doesn't matter. What's important is the food on your plate."

"Are you going to force-feed me?" he asked, his voice revealing amazement and annoyance.

After a while though, he started to nibble at the soup their good friend Anne Allman had prepared specially for him. He was not the kind of man to disappoint his wife!

Nancy's efforts eventually bore fruit and her worries decreased as Ronnie recovered his appetite and his fever subsided subsequently. The broad-spectrum antibiotics Nancy had feared so much probably helped too.

Now he was the one who was getting worried for his spouse and begged her to go home to get a good long sleep.

On April 11, twelve days after he had been shot, the president walked out of the hospital, accompanied by his wife Nancy and his daughter Patti. He was wearing a red cardigan sweater over a bulletproof vest. On the front steps of GW, nurses waved him goodbye and cried. Back in the White House, the entire staff, some two hundred people, were waiting for him in the Rose Garden. They greeted him as a true American hero. Triumphantly. He raised his left arm instinctively as every time he saw a crowd. No doubt, for a fleeting moment, the Hilton pictures crossed his mind.

The public had never known how serious his condition had been. Without Parr's prompt decision to send him to GW when seeing him spit up blood, he probably would have died or had a stroke. "If five minutes had been lost," Dr. Gens had said, "he would have died."[3]

During the whole stay at the hospital, Nancy had carefully managed her husband's image in the media. She did not want him to look tired and would not allow pictures to be taken. Only under growing pressure from the media demanding evidence that his recovery was in compliance with the optimistic hospital releases did she accept that a photograph be taken. Otherwise, all kind of speculation might have been appeared suggesting that the family and medical authorities were hiding the truth about the American president. But the First Lady saw to it that no tube could be seen. The official photograph featuring Nancy holding Ronnie's right arm was in fact carefully airbrushed out to remove a tube protruding from his robe. The nurse standing on the president's left side holding the collection chamber for fluid draining from his chest was also removed from the picture.

This was part of the political game Nancy was playing to preserve her husband. She had meticulously screened the visits at the hospital because she knew the implications some comments could have. Rumor could run so fast. Also, she made sure that Ronnie's previously planned schedule would be postponed only if absolutely necessary. Hence the state visit of Mexican president Lopez Portillo was postponed to until Ronnie's convalescence was totally over.

As a matter of fact, the president had trouble with his breathing and needed a portable respirator for a while, which was known only within the close circle of friends and White House aides. For three weeks, his schedule remained quite limited: he could not conduct more than two meetings each morning, one with the troika, and one with the National Security Council (N.S.C.). The only outside visitor he received during that period, on his request, was that of Cardinal Terence J. Cooke of the Archdiocese of New York. Though it was Good Friday, the clergyman had cancelled his schedule and taken the first plane to the capital. For one hour, the two men stayed together in the Yellow Oval Room, the one reserved to meet heads of state on their first visit. Michael Deaver, who waited outside,

---

[3] *Ibid.*, p. 320.

heard the president say: "I have decided that whatever time I have left is left for Him."[4]

On Easter Monday, the White House hosted its traditional egg roll, a practice initiated by another First Lady, Dolley Madison, in the nineteenth century. The South Lawn is invaded by four-year-olds and parents are allowed "only if accompanied by a child." Nancy brought her personal touch this year by having colored wooden eggs signed by Congressmen, Cabinet officers and ambassadors.

Joy was back and life in the White House was gradually humming at full speed again. Ronnie emerged from his ordeal with renewed strength and determination to implement his political program, in compliance with the ideas for which he had been elected as leader of the nation. His first public appearance took place in Notre Dame where, with cap and gown on, he received an honorary degree and a long standing ovation. He did not feel any better than on those occasions when he knew that he was 100% popular. But his smile was more meaningful this time, it marked the pure enjoyment of being alive and free.

Back in Washington, he was greeted by thunderous applause before a joint session of Congress to defend his Economy Recovery Program bill. His supply-side trickle-down economics theory had been derided by detractors as "Reaganomics", a program that would "reward the rich and screw the poor." But Congress passed both his budget bill and tax bill. The vote was received as an enormous step ahead by the president and his Cabinet. A major obstacle had been overcome and the road was now clear to put political theory into practice.

It seemed that the attempted assassination boosted the president's popularity and weakened opposition. He acquired a new dimension, a grander status. For a while, there had been doubts about the president's ability to govern because of his age. He had also been criticized as a superficial politician, a constant manipulator, a mediocre Hollywood actor, a great but shallow communicator. The biggest criticism, surely, was that he was dim! Now all these grievances seemed to have vanished of their own accord. The public responded with admiration to his survival. Other presidents had died. Ronald Reagan was stronger and in a religious country like America, there was also the thought that the hand of God had saved him.

If the president had emerged stronger from the March 30 ordeal, it was his wife who seemed to suffer the most emotional exhaustion from it all. The fear of losing her husband, the continuous worrying about his health, her doubts about the decisions of the medical corps, the pressure from the press had taken its toll on

---

[4] Michael K. Deaver, *Behind The Scenes – In which the author talks about Ronald and Nancy Reagan...and himself* (New York: William Morrow & Co., 1987), p. 26.

her. She seemed to be weak and out of touch. She was harrowed by her own insecurities again. Her dream of perfection was shattered. The state of shock had generated anxiety, fear and apprehension. Her memory could not dismiss the painful moments, and horrible images and thoughts recurrently crossed her mind. She often kept quiet and when she spoke, she could not use the words "assassination" or "shooting", referring instead to "the thing that happened to Ronnie" or "March thirtieth". The only certainty she had was her awareness of how limited her control of her husband's life had become. For this reason, privately, she called astrologer Joan Quigley in San Francisco and hired her to chart her husband's daily horoscope and obtain advice on scheduling his itinerary every time he had to leave the White House. In May, Maureen was getting married in Beverly Hills to Dennis Revell whom she had met eight years before while working as California Young Republicans, but the presidential couple did not attend their daughter's third marriage. The First Lady refused. March thirtieth was the excuse. Ron and Patti were not among the four hundred guests either.

The psychological effects also produced physical trouble on Nancy. She lost 10 pounds in the weeks that followed the "thing". She was five feet four and her weight slipped from 114 pounds to a rather gaunt 104. Some congratulated her for looking like a mannequin and asked about the secret of her slim figure: "Just have your husband go into politics!" she would reply. And now the irony was seeing the president worry about his wife. "He's always telling me to get some rest and eat more. He tells me that all the time."

The press started to lash at Nancy again, blaming her for her whims and moody nature and paranoia, antagonizing on her never doing anything right. Through a much tried and tested technique, the media targeted the First Lady partly because, with the recent events, they could not decently hit at the president.

On May 1, Nancy's schedule featured a "private" dinner for Prince Charles in the White House living quarters. What the press related most in its columns was the curtsy Lee Annenberg, the American Chief of Protocol, made to the prince upon his arrival in Washington. What appears as a mark of reverence and civility in England was denounced as un-American, some comments judging it indecent in memory of those ancestors who had fought the War of Independence. Diana Vreeland, the former editor of *Vogue*, one of the long social guest list, was photographed also curtsying to Prince Charles. Eyebrows were raised as Nancy appeared standing at her side, with a wholehearted smile, regardless of popular

American culture. "It was as if Nancy Reagan were saying to the country: I am going to do what I want to do," wrote Marie Brenner in *New York* magazine.[5]

The Prince Charles party was followed by a luncheon given by the Congressional Club, wives of congressmen, in honor of Nancy. Frank Sinatra was the surprise guest or rather the "gift" they offered her on that May day. The First Lady admitted that she had always had a crush on "Francis Albert." After the assassination attempt, he was a regular visitor at the White House, using his own Secret Service code name, "Napoleon." He sang some of her favorite songs and when it was over, she rushed into his arms and hugged him tenderly. The ladies were a bit disappointed to see Nancy skip out with Sinatra before the end of the whole program and protocol. She was blamed for "breaking rank", another great paradox of a First Lady who usually did not tolerate breaking the rules of etiquette. But this time, there was Ole Blue Eyes . . .

The royal wedding of Prince Charles and Lady Diana Spencer took place in July. For several weeks, Nancy had had nothing to talk about but the historic British event. Because he was too busy, Ronnie did not go and for the first time in their marriage, Nancy would be away from him for a whole week. She took along an armada of escorts including her dear friends Betsy and Alfred Bloomingdale, eighteen attendants among whom her personal hairdresser Julius Bengtsson, her maid Anita, an official photographer, four members of her staff, Secret Service agents and a dozen reporters. Her gift to the royal couple was a $75,000 glass bowl that the Steuben Glass Company had discounted to 8,000 for the occasion. It was revealed that Nancy's royal wardrobe included twenty different dresses and gowns. She brought a $250,000 Bulgari set of diamond and ruby necklace with matching earrings and rings. Oh, and there was also the diamond necklace she had worn at the Inaugural, the one designed by Harry Winston. In five days she attended no fewer than fifteen social events, including a party at the American embassy where she was the guest of honor, tea with the Queen Mother, lunch at Chequers with Prime Minister Margaret Thatcher, a ball at Buckingham Palace, an invitation to the country estate of Jack and Dru Heinz, the ketchup millionaires, a dinner given by Princess Alexandra and a polo match for which occasion she was introduced to Lady Di by the best player himself, Prince Charles.

If Nancy was lashed at by the press at home, she was not spared criticism overseas either. The British media attacked her for her failure to observe such a time-honored tradition as bowing or curtsying to the queen. The Saturday morning press mocked her wealthy snobbish entourage and grotesque six-vehicle

---

[5] Bob Colacello, « Ronnie and Nancy : The White House Years and Beyond », *Vanity Fair*, August 1998, p. 169.

motorcade. The London *Times* referred to her trying to get "more engagements into the week before the royal wedding than Alice's white rabbit."[6] The *Guardian* made unflattering comments on her very brief insignificant movie career and a caricature portrayed the First Lady wearing a crown.

Sitting among the 2,500 privileged guests at St Paul's Cathedral on July 30, 1981, Nancy watched the wedding of Prince Charles and Lady Diana with infinite admiration. Here was British pomp and circumstance at its best, a lavish display of wealth, color, beauty and tradition that celebrated one of the most wonderful fairy-tale romances of the century. She felt privileged indeed, close to being a royal herself.

Back in the States, Nancy was so happy to meet her Ronnie and tell him every detail of that wonderful stay with the British monarchy. Ronnie was pleased that his wife had enjoyed herself. The experience had had a therapeutic effect on her mind. A week later, the First Couple left Washington for the first of their annual one-month vacations at Rancho Del Cielo in California. They both needed a good rest.

They had got off to a trying seven month start in the White House but for Nancy in particular, worse was to come. It was her extravagant lifestyle and luxurious tastes that sparked off the spate of criticism.

First, Prince Charles's wedding had fuelled the antagonisms. The same facts brought the same effects on either side of the Atlantic. National papers vilified the American First Lady for all the money she had spent on clothes and jewels and parties, along with her wealthy friend Betsy Bloomingdale, for the cost of her escort and for her queenly airs. Nancy's British queen caricature soon found an American replica in the form of a postcard designed by Alfred Gescheidt, caricaturing Mrs. Reagan in a crown and ermine robes and which, at ninety-five cents a piece, sold out in a few weeks. "Queen Nancy" postcards and posters appeared just about everywhere and amused foreign tourists as much as American citizens. Yet if the former laughed at the picture, the latter rather sneered.

It did not help either that the presidential California vacation cost American tax payers a princely quarter of a million dollars.

But the real problems came with Nancy's decision to start a massive renovation of the private quarters of the White House. After the gloomy Carter years, Nancy's primary goal was to restore style and glamour into the mansion and more generally into the presidency. She had a half-million budget but needed more, a lot more. She saw herself as the Jacky Kennedy of the eighties bringing back Camelot's glitter to the White House. Confident that hers was a noble

---

[6] Leamer, op. cit., p. 340.

endeavor, she raised funds through private donations, by persuading her wealthy connections and corporations to donate money for the improvements needed. The $800,000 she received helped pay the new furniture, curtains, wallpaper as well as the new carpeting and reupholstering of antiques. Ted Graber was given the redecoration mission. Elegance was a real concern. Once the embellishment work was over, Nancy let *Architectural Digest* have the exclusive photo rights of the magnificent interiors. The December 1981 issue presented eighteen pages of color pictures and became a collector's edition.

Though the money was not directly spent from public funds, the press did attack the First Lady, arguing that the funding package smacked of conflict of interest. Indeed the donated money was tax deductible from tax returns in the 50 percent tax bracket. In other words, money *did* come, although indirectly, from the public treasury. The furor increased when it was revealed that $270,000 had been raised from oil interests in Texas and Oklahoma, less than a month after Reagan had removed control on oil prices.

This altogether luxurious renovation contrasted sharply and almost indecently with the difficulties of "the real world." Every day, the press was crammed with ever more alarming reports about the recession, rising unemployment and urban homelessness.

Nancy was particularly hurt by an article in the *Washington Post* in which Judy Mann wrote that regardless of the economic situation, "Nancy Reagan has used the position, her position to improve the quality of life for those in the White House."[7]

When on September 3 the White House announced the purchase of a new set of formal china, the "Queen Nancy" image became a more obvious and cruel symbol of her ignorance, or contempt, of the common man's every day preoccupations. The new "Nancy-red" 4,732-piece set of ivory china was worth $209,508; each of its 220 place settings, embossed with the presidential seal in gold, cost about $1,000. Nancy defended herself and explained that it came from a donor who wished to stay anonymous. As the controversy was hotting up, the donor soon revealed her name to release the pressure on the First Lady. It was Antoinette Vojvoda of the Knapp Foundation from Maryland who had purchased the china and honored the White House with the precious gift. Nancy repeated time and again, "I did not buy the china". But the more she defended her position, the more trouble she ran into with the media and a growing number of Americans. Mrs. Reagan was seen as a wealthy selfish woman living in her ivory (china!)

---

[7] Nancy Reagan, with William Novak, *My Turn: the Memoirs of Nancy Reagan* (New York: Random House, 1989), p. 27.

tower totally insulated from the economic crisis that was hitting the country. Washingtonians had a bad joke about it all making fun of Reagan's three China policies: the Taiwan, China, policy; the Mainland China policy; and Nancy's china policy. Even Ronald was lampooned for accepting another superfluous luxurious gift: a pair of ostrich hide cowboy boots. At the same time, the administration proposed a $41 billion cut in welfare programs. Years later, Nancy confessed that the timing of the acquisition had been unfortunate: "The New White House china was announced on the same day that the Department of Agriculture mistakenly declared tomato ketchup to be acceptable as a vegetable for school lunches. As you can imagine, the columnists and the cartoonists had a field day with that one."[8] Yes, to many all this brought evidence that the administration was insensitive to problems of working people and the poor. Even (underprivileged) children had to endure the vagaries of those in charge of public policy. Ironically, it was revealed that the president's least favorite vegetable happened to be . . . tomatoes!

The media inveighed against Nancy not only because of her deco and china. She was also derided for her excessive interest in clothes. The image portrayed was that of a fashion-obsessed woman wearing expensive designer dresses twenty-four hours a day. Her $10,000 Inauguration gown had sparked off criticism. But she kept receiving more gowns, coats, suits from prominent designers like Bill Blass, James Galanos, Adolfo, David Haynes and Jean Louis. Again, she explained those were gifts or had been accepted on loan for special occasions. But soon the International Revenue Service investigated whether all these loans that she had failed to return violated the 1977 Ethics in Government Act, which required her to report them. Though Mrs. Reagan argued that the donation process was an undisputed common practice in Europe, boosting the fashion industry, she ended up donating the clothes to museums. It was later discovered that she did donate a couple of them, with much publicity, but very soon accepted loans again. Sardonic reports in the press mentioned that only one of Mrs. Reagan's handbags cost more than a full year's provision of food stamps for a family of four!

By the end of 1981, Nancy had the highest disapproval rating of all modern time First Ladies. Only Mary Todd Lincoln, the Civil War First Lady who went on buying sprees while soldiers died on the battlefields, had been less popular. In early December, an ABC-*Washington Post* poll gave Mrs. Reagan a 23 percent disapproval rating – compared to 18% in June. And two weeks later, on December 22, a *Newsweek* poll found that 66 percent of the population opposed the First

---

[8] *Ibid.*, p. 29.

Lady's conspicuous consumption "during a time of Federal Budget cuts and economic hardships." 61 percent felt that she was less sympathetic to the problems of the poor and the underprivileged than previous First Ladies. Indeed, the recession the country was going through was the worst since the Depression. Contrary to Mr. Reagan's plan, unemployment kept rising to reach almost 9 percent. In big cities like New York, needy people waited in line outside soup kitchens. News was all about 11,400 air-traffic controllers who were fired for going out on strike. Polls did not spare the president as they revealed that 52 percent of the American public saw him as favoring the rich and disregarding the average-income people. The First Couple were likened to their California friends, "millionaires on parade".

Nancy's luxurious taste and supercilious manners gave rise to unpleasant nicknames such as "the Iron Butterfly", "the Cutout Doll", "the Hollywood Princess", "the Belle of Rodeo Drive" and "Fancy Nancy". Bob Hope, supposedly a friend of the Reagans', joked on Nancy's image of luxury saying that her nurse chuckled, "Gucci, Gucci, goo!" Johnny Carson quipped that Nancy's favorite junk food was caviar! In *Ms* magazine, feminist Gloria Steinem called her "the marzipan wife". The New York *Daily News* compared her to a "let-them-eat-cake" Marie-Antoinette. It seemed that every day, she was the target of ever more reporters, columnists and caricaturists from the liberal media, satirizing her wearing too much red, her "piano legs", her being too rich, too snobbish, too conservative.

The president's advisers began regarding her as a political liability. It was suggested that she should seek psychiatric help to analyze and thrash out the image problem. Ronnie's advice was to just relax and joke, just like he did.

In October, Nancy was the guest of honor of the Al Smith Memorial dinner in New York. On such occasions, the tradition was for her to be introduced to the crowd, acknowledge the applause and say a few "thank you so much" words. This time, she remained standing and decided to execute Ronnie's advice and use humor to defuse all the criticism that had pervaded the press in the last few months. She referred to the popular "Queen Nancy" postcard that showed her with a crown on her head.

"Now that's silly. I'd never wear a crown. It messes up your hair," she declared. Then, as the crowd roared, she disclosed the name of her new pet charity: "The Nancy Reagan Home for Wayward China." Again, the room rang out with laughter. Sure now that this audience was all on her side, she made a few comments on the scandal raised by the contributions from friends for redecorating some of the White House rooms. "I'm glad I raised as much as I did for the White House," she said. "Ronnie thinks I did such a good job, he wants me to help work on the deficit."[9] The crowd gave her a sustained standing ovation and she sat down with a genuine smile of satisfaction.

In December she was interviewed by Mike Wallace, an old family friend, on the popular "60 minutes" television program. Nancy was introduced as a caring sensitive First Lady who had been hurt by all the negative press. Wallace offered the American nation to give Mrs. Reagan a "fresh look" for Christmas. "That would be nice," she concluded with an ingratiating smile.

1981 ended with the appointment of Sandra Day O'Connor to the United States Supreme Court, the first woman in the nation's history. Despite the recession, the president was gratified with overall good marks in public opinion. Tax cuts and an increase in defense spending received the support of a majority of Americans. For Nancy, there was a glimmer of hope after months of worries, contempt and incomprehension. Now was the time for a fresh start.

---

[9] « The World of Nancy Reagan, » *Newsweek*, December 21, 1981, p. 25.

Part V

FIRST LADY: "HIGH HIGHS AND LOW LOWS"[1]

"Last year was a lost year," Nancy was reported to have said in early 1982.[2]

At Camp David, East Wing and West Wing staffers met to analyze Nancy's problems and find a way to revamp her image because it was becoming a political liability to the president. . . . The 1984 presidential campaign was already looming. Nancy's image had to be turned into an asset. Deaver brought in a new chief of staff, thirty-two-year-old James Rosebush, to lead the rehabilitation campaign. After long discussions weighing up the different ideas and propositions, the presidential advisers elaborated a three-pronged strategy.

First, the First Lady had to keep away from her California friends for a while and give up the appearance of frivolity and extravagance by toning down the glamorous parties and couturier dresses.

Second, she had to turn the fickle media from foes into friends. Not an easy enterprise.

Sheila Tate, Nancy's press secretary, proposed that the First Lady appear at the Gridiron Dinner, an annual white-tie event put on by an élite club of 60 journalists for Washington power-brokers including the president, prominent politicians and journalists. On March 27, at the Capital Hilton Hotel, Ronnie and Nancy sat among the 600 guests of the ritual gathering. One of the highlights of the evening was a lampoon on the First Lady. A skit, based on a hit song of the 1920s, "Secondhand Rose from Second Avenue" by Fanny Brice, parodied Mrs. Reagan's taste for designer clothes:

---

[1] Nancy Reagan, about her years in the White House. In « Nancy Reagan Defends Her Right in Advising the President », *The New York Times*, 5 May 1987, p. A26.

[2] *New York Times*, 19 February 1982, p. B5. Quoted in Gil Troy, *Affairs of State* (New York: Free Press, 1997), p. 288.

Second-hand clothes.
I give my second-hand clothes
To museum collections and travelling shows.
They were oh so happy that they got 'em,
Won't notice they were ragged at the bottom.
Goodbye, you old, worn-out mess.
I never wear a frock more than once.
Calvin Klein, Adolfo, Ralph Lauren
And Bill Blass.
Ronald Reagan's mama's going strictly
First Class.
Rodeo Drive. I sure miss Rodeo Drive
In frumpy Washington.

Second-hand rings.
Donate those old, used-up things.
Designers deduct 'em.
We're living like kings.
So what if Ronnie's cutting back on welfare?
I'll still wear a tiara in my coiffed hair.

Before the thunderous applause even came to an end, Nancy slipped out of the room. Those who had seen the scene thought she had left upset by the satire. Suddenly the crowd couldn't believe their eyes when a raggedly and clownishly dressed woman appeared on stage. She wore a red straw hat with feathers, a blue print aqua skirt and a flowery shirt fastened with safety pins, a long double strand of faked pearls, a white feather boa and yellow hillbilly rubber boots. Soon the audience realized the outré sitcom bag lady was the First Lady in person! Holding a china plate in her hand, she started singing her own version of Fanny Brice's ditty with lyrics that had been rewritten by East Wing staff members for the occasion:

I'm wearing second-hand clothes,
Second-hand clothes.
They're quite the style
In spring fashion shows.
Even my new trench coat with fur collar
Ronnie bought for ten cents on the dollar.
Second-hand gowns

And old hand-me-downs,
The china is the only thing that's new.
Even though they tell me that I'm no longer
Queen,
Did Ronnie have to buy me that new
Sewing machine?
Second-hand clothes, second-hand clothes,
I sure hope Ed Meese sews.

She then kicked off her rubber boots and broke the ignominious china-looking plate for a smashing finale that brought down the house. Never in her stage career had she received such an ovation and so many cheers and shouts of "bravo" and "encore". The unexpected self-deprecating performance impressed the Washington media and became headline news. Even the *New York Times* applauded: "No other Fist Lady had ever come so well prepared with shtick, even including a mock piece of White House china to smash onstage. Socko!"[3] The *Washington Post* related the story with a flattering headline: "First Lady Steals Show at Annual Gridiron Dinner." All the press reviews paid tribute to Nancy's ability to laugh at herself. The performance undoubtedly marked a turnaround in the First Lady's relations with the press. It transformed her in the public eye. People saw a different side of her. Now they loved her.

In June, the presidential couple flew overseas and went the rounds of European capitals: Paris, where Ronnie attended the economic summit in the Versailles palace; Rome, where they visited Pope John Paul II at the Vatican; London, featuring a royal banquet at Windsor with Queen Elizabeth and Prince Phillip; Bonn, Germany, which hosted an important NATO meeting. Despite a few criticisms of Nancy's gaffes (she had cancelled a visit to a children's cancer clinic at the last minute to take three hours to rest before the Windsor dinner), extravagant wardrobe (some of the 1981 lessons had still to be learned) and inappropriate selections of dresses (wearing black satin knickers and a tunic, she looked "*très gauche*" in Paris!), the trip turned out to be a true success. As the couple arrived in Washington, they were greeted by a cheering crowd of fifteen thousand well-wishers to whom the White House had offered free tickets for the arrival ceremony.

But soon sorrow and sadness took the upper hand and Nancy was feeling low again as she was hit by successive blows. First, their friend Alfred Bloomingdale

---

[3] Bill Adler, *Ronnie and Nancy: A Very Special Love Story* (New York: Crown Publishers, 1985), p. 190.

was involved in a sex scandal that gave the tabloid press enough matter to chew on. He was sued for $5 million in palimony by Vicki Morgan, a twenty-seven year old playgirl, thirty-six years younger than him, who claimed she had been his "traveling companion" –read "mistress"– since the age of seventeen and he had been paying her $18,000 a month. But now he was dying and could not even sign checks.

Nancy's father, Dr. Loyal, "Bopa", was in hospital with a serious heart problem and his condition was declining every day. But Nancy's first encounter with death that summer was quite an unexpected one. Ed and Ursula Meese's son, Scott, was killed in a car accident. He was a freshman at Princeton. Both Ronnie and Nancy were extremely affected by the death of the nineteen-year-old boy whom they had known since his early childhood. Then as they mourned over Scott, on August 19, 1982, Dr. Loyal died. In the Phoenix hospital, Nancy had stayed at his side till he breathed his last. The very next day, Alfred Bloomingdale died. And less than a month later, Princess Grace of Monaco was killed in a car crash, and Nancy flew to the principality to attend the funeral of the ex-Hollywood actress.

Nancy was devastated by these successive deaths, especially Dr. Loyal's, and remained depressive for a few weeks. To crown it all, she had a cancer removed from her lip.

If Dr. Davis's death grieved the First Lady most sincerely, her close friends noted that it also strengthened her sway over the president. Indeed, Ronnie, whose perception of Nancy was always that of the sweetest woman and most adoring wife, now cared for her every second and attended to her every need. He would seldom contradict her for fear he would hurt her feelings. Whether this were a cunning stratagem or not, or a vaguely conscious privilege, it would grant Nancy more open access to White House affairs, strengthen her authority and consolidate her position of influence.

The third constituent of Nancy's makeover as designed by Deaver and Rosebush was for the First Lady to have a project of her own. All great First Ladies have a noble cause. "Since Eleanor Roosevelt, the public has come to expect only that she use this exalted position to do some good for someone or some cause," observes historian Charles S. Clark.[4] The New Deal First Lady worked on the fronts of social causes and justice and helped the underprivileged, the unemployed or the soldiers based in different countries around the world. But even before her, Ellen Wilson manifested her social conscience by lobbying Congress to pass legislation in favor of Washington's poor black people who

---

[4] Charles S. Clark, « First Ladies », *CQ Researcher,* 14 June 1996, vol. VI, n° 22, p. 522.

lived in dilapidated dwellings. Her "alley bill" was passed in 1914. Grace Coolidge volunteered for the Red Cross, Lou Hoover was president of the Girl Scouts. In the 1960s, Jacky Kennedy used her knowledge of art to initiate a vast restoration project of the White House and created "the White House Historical Association", Lady Bird Johnson was a pioneer of the environmental cause with her "Beautify America!" program and it was under her pressure that in October 1965, the "Highway Beautification Bill" was passed. Rosalynn Carter found her own voice on behalf of senior citizens and the mentally ill, a fight that resulted in the passage of the "Age Discrimination Act" and "Mental Health Systems Act" of 1980.

Soon after Ronnie's election, the dean of the White House press corps, UPI correspondent Helen Thomas, had asked Nancy what her project in the White House would be. "I don't have one," she had answered. "My husband is most important." Her only focus would be her husband and her home.

"You will make a big mistake if you don't pursue any great goal," Thomas had warned, prophetically. By not following this advice, Nancy had estranged herself from the media, which had seen her as a superficial woman, and from career women across the country who rejected her image as a 1950s throwback, unaware of modern women's lives. But 1981 was now behind her and she wanted to start afresh, eager to show the caring side of her personality and to lend her name to public service programs. The truth was she had already been involved in honorable causes even before being installed at the White House. The MIA project and Foster Grandparents program as well as her war on drugs had revealed her capacity to use her name and position to improve the conditions of those who suffered. But these projects, respectable as they were, remained minor accomplishments. In addition, they had attracted criticism and skepticism in the media. How sincere had she been? Hadn't her efforts been political gimmicks as part of her husband's electoral strategy?

Now the White House wanted to seize on her pre-White House action as a way to restore her image and make her appear an activist First Lady. After several meetings, White House officials launched what was known as "Project-Nancy-Has-a-Heart". Reluctant at first, Nancy eventually understood that taking up "a cause of her own" would serve her husband. Any positive action from the First Lady would contribute to the president's popularity and help him implement his political program. So she worked hard to develop "Foster Grandparents" and make it one of her great "social issues." It must be said that this was a traditional and politically safe First Lady project. It was ideal for photo opportunities, with Nancy hugging children and old people. The public liked to see a First Lady who cared for the suffering, particularly when it came to children. Frank Sinatra recorded a song, "To Love a Child", specially for Nancy's project. In October 1982, he was invited to the White House and the celebrated crooner and the First Lady sang the song together before six hundred guests of the grandparents-children program. Nancy also released a book, with the same title, *To Love a Child* that she had co-written with California author Jane Wilkie. The proceeds of the song and the book, both bests sellers, went to Foster Grandparents. She appeared on many television talk-shows during which she publicized the program and polished her image. Her emotional approach to social problems was well received and the Queen-bee Nancy label forgotten. The combined efforts of the First Lady and all the actors of the program seem to have paid off as the 1980s saw Foster Grandparents grow from 16,900 volunteers helping 50,700 children to 26,600 and 66,500 respectively.[5]

She also took on another cause, one she said she cherished with all her heart: drug abuse among young people. Yet Deaver and other White House officials initially feared the issue might confine the First Lady into a negative campaign attacking an unsolvable problem. There was a risk of being accused of incompetence and political manipulation. The administration did not want any conflict with the medical community. Deaver's concerns proved right as Nancy's early opinions on the question remained uncertain and emotional, rather than based on scientific knowledge. Her action soon raised questions on her credibility.

"We have to get marijuana out of the movies," she once said at a luncheon in Georgetown.

One of the women in the room, well-informed on the drug problem, listened in dismay as she realized the First Lady's approach and solutions to the problem were inadequate and very limited.

"If you want to have an effective antidrug program," said the woman whose own children had suffered from drug addiction, "worrying about marijuana in the movies would be counterproductive."[6] Nancy looked disarmed and just grinned and bore it.

The First Lady's early speeches were repetitive and not very convincing. The press was getting bored with covering her visits to drug rehabilitation centers for teen-agers where the same scenes were repeated over and over again: hugs, tears and Nancy saying: "My heart is filled with so many things I'd like to say to you, if I can get through them. I'm so proud of you and I love you, too."[7]

[5] Troy, op. cit., p. 289.
[6] Laurence Leamer, *Make-Believe: The Story of Nancy & Ronald Reagan* (New York: Harper and Row, 1983), p. 334.
[7] *Ibid.*, p. 358.

A satirical column, "Ask Nancy", which appeared in the December 1982 issue of *Drug Survival News*, a magazine specializing on drug, alcohol and health information, infuriated the White House, whose Counsel to the President, Mr. Fred F. Fielding, complained to the editor. The latter, Mr. James D. Parker of "Do It Now" publications, wrote back to point out what his intentions had been in writing and publishing the column: "The main goal I sought to achieve in running the column was to contrast the Reagan administration's official policy of budget cuts and fiscal derring-do in the drug abuse field with the unofficial hand-wringing that Mrs. Reagan routinely and publicly performs on the "drug problem". . . . . And rather than doing what can and should be done to rehabilitate the hundreds of thousands of addicts and abusers who guarantee the perpetuation of the drug problem in this country, the administration instead treats us to round after round of budget cuts and program slashes and to the unlikely spectacle of the first lady of the United States mumbling inanities about a complex social problem about which she demonstrates precious little understanding."[8]

Skeptics attacked the project on two fronts: they criticized Mrs. Reagan's lack of grasp of the problem and pointed out that while she was fighting drugs, her husband slashed 26% from the budget for drug prevention and education programs.

Despite the criticisms, Nancy wanted to show she had a sense of high purpose and insisted on working on a project that was close to her heart. She admitted her own children had used drugs. Life on campus in the 1970s and desire for independence had also confronted Patti and Ron with the usage of marijuana. Nancy felt concerned about a scourge that no American family was sheltered from. She strongly denied that federal appropriations would solve the problem and referred to Alcoholic Anonymous as a typical example of a free, independent yet successful organization. She emphasized private morality : "I don't think throwing a lot of money into this problem is going to solve it," she explained. "It's going to be solved by people standing up and taking a position that it is wrong and they won't put up with it. It's morally wrong."[9] She believed in volunteerism and non-profit efforts. Focusing on the essential role of parents, she presented herself as a First Lady who was also a mother and wanted to use her position to help other parents cope with the problem. She told NBC correspondent Chris Wallace that her faith in and encouragement of the parental bond stemmed

---

[8] Letter, James D. Parker to Fred F. Fielding (31 May, 1983), "Drug Survival News Item" folder, box 11421, Peter J. Rusthoven Files, Ronald Reagan Library, Simi Valley, California.
[9] Hugh Sidey, « It's Morally Wrong » , *Time*, 6 October 1986, p. 22.

from the enduring feeling of her own separation from her mother in her early childhood.[10]

Throughout 1982, she crusaded against drug abuse, crisscrossing the country, touring drug prevention and treatment facilities. She enjoyed talking with teenagers, giving them moral support and publicized the testimonies of former addicts. She gave numerous speeches and hosted countless luncheons, including one in Washington where she asked governors' wives to relay her action in their states. She took part in the White House Conference on Drug Use and Families and attended a long series of anti-drug conferences. As the presidential couple traveled to Europe in the summer, she changed part of her social schedule (galas, receptions, etc.) to visit drug rehabilitation centers. The war against drugs increasingly became the First Lady's label. A new image was emerging. To some extent, her anti-drug cause also revealed her influence on her husband as, at her request, the president appointed a task force to deal with the drug problem.

Of course, as a former actress and the wife of a former actor, Mrs. Reagan knew the power of the media and how the whole system worked. She took advantage of her new positive image to raise her profile and spread information on drugs. In 1983, she sang in the chorus of the music video *Stop the Madness* with Los Angeles Lakers basketball star Kareem Abdul-Jabbar and actor Arnold Schwartzenegger; she also honored pop singer Michael Jackson at the White House for his anti-drug activities. She appeared in a cameo role on one episode of NBC's sitcom "Diff'rent Strokes" (March 19, 1983) where she counseled the young child star and his TV classmates against drug abuse. She made an announcement to the year's largest television audience (112 million people) during halftime of Super Bowl XVII, and became the first First Lady to appear on a late-night television talk-show. She co-hosted a full week of ABC's morning show "Good Morning America", and narrated a two-hour documentary on drug abuse, "The Chemical People" for the Public Broadcasting Service.

She lobbied against the illusory glamorization of drugs in modern entertainment and called on TV producers and film-makers to stop portraying pot-smoking scenes in movies and TV dramas and to create characters who clearly showed their opposition to drugs .

The publicity Nancy created forced the nation to address a serious cultural problem.

During 1984, she participated in 110 events for this cause, the closest to her heart. At one of them, which took place in Oakland's Longfellow Elementary

[10] Carl Sferrazza Anthony, *First Ladies: The Saga of the Presidents' Wives and Their Power, Vol. 2, 1961-1990* (New York: Quill/Morrow, 1991), p. 366.

School, one little girl asked: "But Mrs. Reagan, what should I say if someone offers me drugs, if someone wants to give them to me?"

"Just say NO!," Mrs. Reagan answered. "That's all you have to do. Just say no and walk away."[11]

The three-word answer soon became a slogan and throughout the country more than 5,000 "Just Say No to Drugs" clubs were launched by young people to fight drugs at the peer level.

At each of her visits to schools and youth groups, the question was a ritual:

"What should you do when someone offers you drugs?"

"Just say no!" the teenage crowd would reply.

"What will you do when someone offers you drugs?"

"Just say no!"

In 1985, her international reputation as an anti-drug campaigner was established when she invited eighteen First Ladies from other countries to a historic two-day drug summit in Washington and Atlanta. That same year, she hosted an unprecedented session for "First Ladies" from thirty countries at the United Nations' fortieth anniversary. It was the first time in history that an incumbent president's wife addressed the U.N. She also had a private audience with the Pope about drug abuse.

The campaign to improve Nancy's image had worked wonderfully and succeeded beyond all expectations. Her project was regarded as the most successful in First Lady history. By May 1986, as five million people participated in "Just Say No" marches organized in seven hundred cities, she had traveled about one hundred thousand miles, appeared on more than twenty talk shows, given 1,254 media interviews, and delivered forty-nine speeches.

Although the war against drugs was not won – can never be won – drug and alcohol addiction among students dropped from one third to one fourth. By 1985, almost three quarters of high school seniors surveyed called marijuana harmful. The drug-happy spirit of the 1960s and 1970s seemed less popular or at least less attractive among young people.[12]

The fight against drugs was typical of Nancy's ambiguous role. Originally, her action had been the instrument of a political strategy initiated by East Wing and West Wing aides. Her success resulted from a public relations campaign that had been planned to emphasize her compliance with the public expectations of what the proper role of a First Lady should be: warm, caring and compassionate. The construction of this positive image was supposed to rebound favorably on the

---

[11] Frances Spatz Leighton, *The Search For the Real Nancy Reagan* (New York: Macmillan Publishing Company, 1987), p. 365.

[12] Troy, op. cit., pp. 291-292.

president's popularity. This was not negligible for a woman who always claimed the support of her husband was her top priority. Yet this is only part of the truth as Nancy took her project with earnest devotion. Though her approach might have been denounced as too emotional, too political or too superficial, it cannot be denied that she turned all her energies and attention to a very serious problem among American youth and the only reason why her crusade became so popular was because she undertook it most genuinely and sincerely.

Even the press greeted her crusade with positive coverage. She was presented as "the White House Co-Star" in a cover story of *Time Magazine* (January 14, 1985) and was the guest of an all-positive hour-long special on NBC.

Nancy had emerged as a national moral force which was highly appreciated in the 1980s. The war against permissiveness that Ronald Reagan had promised to lead during his campaign, was taking form under Nancy's leadership. It had the multiple advantages of suiting public opinion as well as conservative aspirations for a moral revolution, without hurting liberal social sensitivity or damaging the president's economic program.

Nancy ranked high in opinion polls and for the first time, her popularity surpassed the president's. In a *New York Times*/CBS poll in January 1985, she obtained a 71% favorability rate against 62% for her husband. His disapproval reached 30%, hers 14%. According to a Wirthlin poll, she was more highly regarded than any member of the president's Cabinet.[13] One of the lowest-rated American First Ladies after one year in the White House, she was now well up at the top of the most admired women list. Project-Nancy-Has-a-Heart was definitely a success and had changed the public's perception of the nation's First Lady. The former élitist image that combined wealth, ostentatious elegance and aloofness had given way to such qualities as compassion, care and understanding. She was no longer surrounded by Californian self-made millionaires but seemed much more involved in "the real world" – she was perceived as much more in touch with average American citizens.

Once a political liability, Nancy had become an asset to the Reagan administration. In 1986, when president Reagan signed anti-drug abuse legislation, he symbolically turned the pen to his wife. The gesture marked his recognition of his wife's action against drugs but also revealed the First Lady's political weight. One *Time* headline read: "Nancy Reagan's clout and causes bring new respect."[14] Indeed, she now seemed to enjoy an aura of respectability that reflected the sense of mission and power that she had acquired since 1982. The

---

[13] Anthony, op. cit., p. 371.
[14] *Time*, 14 January 1985, p. 5.

success of her project became a political plus, as her fame enlarged her circle of friends across the country and made her more influential in the public domain. In addition, the First Lady was not "just the president's wife" but a person in her own right. Though she recognized she was a born worrier, her experience gave her more self-confidence and helped her manage her public and private life less anxiously. She delivered speeches more frequently and more effectively. She appeared as comfortable hugging a young addict in a California rehabilitation center as shaking hands with Chinese Leader Deng Xiaoping who, during the Reagans' visit in Peking in the spring of 1984, suggested that "next time" the First Lady "come alone." While the president was in Bonn for an economic summit in May 1985, the main topic of discussion at the state dinner was Mrs. Reagan's drug crusade. "Never have I seen my summit partners as united on a single subject," Reagan told staffers.[15] On a side trip to Rome, she had a private audience with Pope John Paul II who congratulated her and encouraged her in her war on drugs.

But there was more to Nancy's political clout than protocol and photo opportunities. Her influence on her husband became more visible and she played an increasingly powerful role within the administration

In August 1984, at Rancho Del Cielo, an impromptu press conference took place that highlighted both the difficult Soviet-American situation and Nancy's power on her husband. The Reagans were vacationing at the ranch trying to get a breath of fresh air away from the Washington political and media arena. But this is hardly how it turned out. Nancy was fuming to find photographers or reporters swarming everywhere. Even at the top of this mountain, it seemed impossible to get rid of the press. CNN's Charles Bierbauer asked Ronald if there was any hope of seeing the Soviets come to the negotiating table on arms control. The question surreptitiously highlighted a growing rumor about the president's inertia on this particular issue.

"What?" said Ronald hesitatingly.

Bierbauer repeated his question. Nancy, who sensed the danger, came to her husband's rescue whispering, "Doing everything we can." She believed the remark was made out of the earshot of reporters.

"We're doing everything we can," repeated the seventy-three-year-old president.

Unfortunately for the Reagans, one of the CNN microphones recorded Nancy's prompt. She claimed she was not trying to cue her husband but just talking to herself, which of course did not convince anybody.

---

[15] *Time*, 13 May 1985, p. 16.

"The whole Russian affair", as Nancy referred to it years later, started with high tension between East and West, largely between the Soviet Union and the United States. In his first two years at the White House, Reagan had pushed through the most massive military spending ever in peacetime. He had deployed a whole arsenal of missiles and installed Pershing II missiles in NATO countries to counter the SS-20 the Soviets had placed in Eastern Europe. He ordered the production of the B-1 bomber which his predecessor had given up. In March 1983, he initiated his Strategic Defense Initiative (SDI). Star Wars, as it was popularly known, was a sophisticated program to develop a defense system against incoming nuclear missiles. But simultaneously opposition to this race to nuclear arms was widespread. From coast to coast, huge meetings and concerts were organized to denounce the excessive defense budget and the potential risk of a nuclear war. Even Patti Davis, Ronald and Nancy's daughter, was seen on stage at the Rose Bowl in Pasadena, California, in the company of Bob Dylan and Joan Baez, raging against the American nuclear policy.

The White House tried to plead its good faith by claiming that only a strong country could ensure peace. The Administration also argued that there would be no summit between the two countries until the Russians agreed to ease their restrictive emigration policies and repression against political opponents and to show signs of good will in arms control.

Nancy, who was all in favor of improving the relationships between the two superpowers, thought Ronald's toughness against the Soviet Union was politically counterproductive. Therefore she goaded him into softening his "evil empire" speeches. One of these in particular, delivered during a convention of the National Association of Evangelicals in Florida on March 8, 1983, had raised strong indignation. He had called the Soviet Union "the focus of evil in the modern world."

She also worked behind the scenes to break the deadlock and bring about a summit. But the White House was riven by a power struggle between the ideologues, anti-Soviet hardliners, and the more moderate pragmatists like secretary of state George Schultz.

According to Helene Von Damm, Ronnie's former personal secretary and assistant, Nancy and Schultz secretly arranged for the Soviet ambassador Anatoly Dobrynin to meet Reagan in the White House in February. Neither National Security Adviser Bill Clark nor anyone in the West Wing or the press had known. Historian Carl Sferrazza Anthony emphasizes Mrs. Reagan's role in this important diplomatic meeting by saying that the ambassador was smuggled in through the East Wing, a metaphor of the First Lady's power.

Determined as she was, Nancy would not let the ideologues in the White House dictate foreign policy. Here, as in other matters, she was identified as having played a key behind the scenes role in the firings of National Security Adviser William Clark, replaced by Robert "Bud" McFarlane, and Interior Secretary James Watt who had been "forced to resign" (October 1983).[16]

A year and a half later, on September 28, 1984, Nancy was in the White House with her husband, Secretary of State George Shultz and National Security Adviser Bud McFarlane to greet Foreign Minister Andrei Gromyko for the first public reception of a Kremlin leader in the Reagan Administration. Before the working lunch, the Soviet official had a private conversation with the First Lady in the Red Room:

"Does your husband believe in peace?", he asked.

"Yes, of course," Nancy answered.

"Then whisper 'peace' in your husband's ear every night."

Nancy looked at him straight in the eye: "I will, and I'll also whisper it in *your* ear."[17]

The anecdote is one of Nancy's favorites about her White House years. The truth is it was more than just an anecdote and reflected her genuine determination to work for world peace. Of course, she saw the quest for peace as a noble endeavor and believed that great nations had to pursue it for the benefit of the whole world; but she also understood that ending the Cold War would give her husband *the* greatest opportunity to go down in history. She wanted the public to continue adoring Ronnie as she did and the world to remember him as the great peacemaker of the century. "Nancy believed this was her husband's destiny: a man of his age who had lived through two World Wars would be the one to break the deadlock of the Cold War," Mike Deaver observed in an interview to author Kati Marion.[18]

Meanwhile, the presidential election campaign was in full swing and throughout Nancy played an active role fundraising, building coalitions, often participating in strategy meetings and sharing her views about issues and voters' preoccupations with the presidential top advisors. She became a rugged campaigner and unlike in 1976 and 1980, felt quite comfortable in her speeches. She traveled extensively across the country to defend her husband's policies, in particular what was known as "Reaganomics", a program she said had reduced

---

[16] Leighton, op. cit., p. 341.

[17] *Ibid.*, p. 323; Troy, op. cit., p. 297.

[18] Kati Marion, *Hidden Power: Presidential Marriages That Shaped Our Recent History* (New York: Pantheon Books, 2001), p. 254.

unemployment and would result in great prosperity. She protested vehemently against the idea that the Republican Party was only for the rich, and accused Walter Mondale, Ronnie's opponent of unfair play. The Democratic candidate, aged fifty-six, had referred to the president's age, seventy-three, as a handicap, insinuating his capacity to lead the country was diminished. Mrs. Reagan retorted this statement would be felt as an insult by the great number of senior citizens in America. The president himself had turned the matter to his advantage in the second public debate at the end of the campaign: "I will not make age an issue of this campaign. I am not going to exploit, for political purposes, my opponent's youth and inexperience."[19]

The first debate between the two candidates on October 7 1984 had resulted in Reagan going down in the polls and Mondale judged to be the undisputed winner. Ronald complained that his preparation had been "brutalizing", overloaded with statistics and position papers eventually hindering rather than helping his performance. Nancy was upset that her husband's staff had not been able to prepare him efficiently and capitalize on his natural oratorical qualities. She therefore suggested a new approach, advising Deaver to return to the "single speech" method rather than an endless exposé built from multiple texts and sources and overblown with information the president had to memorize. What particularly worried her was that Ronald seemed to be losing his power of concentration and his sense of humor.

As the team were practicing for the second debate at Camp David, the First Lady popped in, walked over to Ronnie and interrupted the rehearsal. In a very un-Nancy-like manner, she suddenly threw open her coat in front of him flashing a "4 MORE IN '84" red sweater and shut it. Taken by surprise, the president and his staff could not believe their eyes. She repeated the scene and everyone burst into laughter. Humor was not known as Nancy's best quality and for everyone present that day the vision seemed surreal: this usually worried and anxious woman was suddenly cheering up her usually jovial and optimistic husband.

The reversal of the roles, unexpected though it was, reflected Nancy's unfailing encouragement for Ronald and unerring conviction that his destiny as the leader of the nation needed more than a fleeting four years. Only in another term would it reach its full effectiveness. She would later work actively – though unsuccessfully – with Republican supporters in favor of the abolition of the 1951 twenty-second amendment to the constitution limiting the presidency to a maximum of two four-year terms. Her performance lifted up Ronnie's spirits. He recovered his concentration and power to communicate, and the debate

---

[19] Leighton, op. cit., p. 302.

preparation continued in a much more relaxed and optimistic atmosphere. The second debate turned out to be a total success for Reagan who won the November election by a landslide, with 59 percent of the popular vote, representing 54.2 million votes against 37.2 million for his opponent. Only one state, Minnesota – Mondale's home state – and Washington D. C. voted for the Democratic candidate. Ronald Reagan received a sweeping 525 electoral votes. He was the oldest candidate to win a presidential election in American history.

The First Lady's political role in the United States was the focus of great attention. Rightly so as her political power became strikingly apparent during her husband's second term. The question was not so much whether Nancy exercised power as how much power she exercised. Reagan himself admitted that Nancy had a strong influence over him, for instance on the U. S.-Soviet relations, by "persuading me to lower the temperature of my rhetoric."[20] True, after helping him maintain a high degree of popularity during the first term, the First Lady now wanted her husband to appear as a man of peace. He had four years to succeed in this thorny but wholly worthwhile enterprise.

Thinking the Geneva summit in November 1985 would be the ideal time to bring the Soviets to the negotiating table, Nancy worked with Shultz and McFarlane, the pragmatists, to set the stage for an historic encounter. She instructed chief of staff Jim Baker to give Ronnie enough latitude to do "his stuff". "Work this out", she insisted, "so Ronnie gets a chance to sit down with Gorbachev."[21] When the American president and the new Russian leader Mikhail Gorbachev met in the Swiss capital, there was an instant cordiality between the two men, a feeling that had never before been experienced in the history of Soviet-American relations. Reagan later confessed that contrary to his cold grim-faced communist predecessors, who had died within a few months of each other over a period of one and a half years (Leonid Brezhnev on November 10, 1982, Yuri Andropov on February 9, 1983 and Konstantin Chernenko on March 10, 1984), the 54-year-old Soviet secretary-general looked warm and friendly. The picture of the two leaders standing hand in hand went around the globe and perfectly suited Nancy's goal of seeing her Ronnie in the history books. On the afternoon of the first day, the two men took a break from the formal talks and had a private meeting in a cozy beach house about a hundred yards away from Fleur d'Eau, the nineteenth-century château overlooking Lake Leman, where the summit was held. The fireside chat, scheduled to last fifteen minutes, ran for an hour and twenty minutes. Of course all the problems were not solved during this

---

[20] Anthony, op. cit., p. 375.
[21] Marion, op. cit., p. 266.

tête-à-tête, but it was an important stage in the negotiations and the two leaders agreed to make plans for two more summits, one in Washington and another one in Moscow. Now Nancy's dream seemed to be on the verge of becoming a reality: her husband had established a "personal working relationship" with Gorbachev – though no agreement was reached in Geneva – and the peace process was firmly on track.

The atmosphere between the two First Ladies was not as cheerful as between their husbands! Nancy did not feel very comfortable in the company of Raisa Maksimovna Titorenko, Mrs. Gorbachev, whom the Russians called "the Czarina." Though Raisa was a truly elegant and cultivated woman, Nancy took a dislike to her right from the start. Raisa, a former teacher, had lectured on Marxist philosophy at Moscow State University. Now she began lecturing Nancy about the virtues of Communism and the greatness of the Soviet Empire. Nancy was disappointed that they did not discuss personal matters: marriage, children, philanthropic activities, or plans for the future. Raisa ignored Nancy's drug program because "there was no drug problem in the Soviet Union." "Her conversational style made me bristle," Nancy wrote in *My Turn*. Raisa talked on and on, glorifying her country and not hesitating to point out the weaknesses and vices of the American political system. Nancy was annoyed by her Soviet counterpart and thought Raisa's First Lady role did not compare with hers. "There isn't even a Russian word for First Lady," Nancy wrote ironically.[22] In public, however, the two women made comments about each other that did not reflect the underlying animosity. They displayed diplomatic propriety and kept up appearances.

In addition to the differences in culture, one of the reasons why Nancy did not get along with Raisa is probably that the Russian played much more than the traditional decorative role of First Lady. She displayed a strong personality and was able to position herself on an equal footing with her White House hostess. Here was a woman of substance, who was intellectually bright and politically clever. Raisa had been the only Soviet leader's wife to play a diplomatic role since Nadezhda Krupskaya, Lenin's wife. Her international visibility was widely commented upon in the world's media. She accompanied her husband just about every time he traveled abroad and was eager to know more about the culture and fashion in the countries they visited.

Yet, compared to Nancy, Mrs. Gorbachev's political role in her country remained extremely limited, in accordance with the lowly place of women in

---

[22] Nancy Reagan, with William Novak, *My Turn: the Memoirs of Nancy Reagan* (New York: Random House, 1989), pp. 337-338.

Russian society at large. When Rosalyn Carter once wanted to accompany her husband in Moscow and attend a meeting with the secretary-general, the former American president was firmly informed that the Russian tradition excluded wives from such meetings in order to maintain an atmosphere of "serious" work. One Soviet official declared: "You see, if Mrs. Carter joins the meeting, then Raisa [Gorbachev] must be included, and then the conference becomes informal and not a discussion in substance."[23]

Nancy and Raisa's first joint appearance before the press marked the start of the rivalry between the two women. Though they were scheduled to appear together and deliver joint messages, Raisa arrived earlier and did not wait for Nancy before answering the reporters' questions. When the U. S. First Lady arrived, she bitterly understood that the Russian lady had relegated her to second place and the atmosphere was most unpleasant. "Who does that dame think she is," the ex-Hollywood actress complained.[24] Yet, her anger remained known only to her close aides and though she genuinely disliked Raisa Gorbachev, Nancy never let her feelings hinder the warming relationships between their two countries. She made a point of voicing her support for the efforts both sides were achieving on the path to peace.

Reagan's second term was unfortunately marked by his growing physical frailty, slipping memory, impaired hearing and incapacity to concentrate for any length of time. These were later seen as early symptoms of Alzheimer's disease. At the same time, Nancy's revamped image and subsequent favorable press coverage facilitated her entry to the corridors of power. Ronald's eternal protector, she became known as the ultimate source of access to the president and a major influence in the White House. This impression was highlighted by a series of crises that agitated the second Reagan administration.

In July 1985, she had to cope with much of the same trauma as after the 1981 assassination attempt. The president was diagnosed as having colon cancer and underwent major surgery. Once again, she had to fight her own fears and the same worries she had endured four years before. Yet she seemed to have matured into a more independent person, and while her husband remained her primary focus, this episode of the presidency revealed how she imposed her authority. She limited communication with the chief executive to the strict minimum and shielded the public and the media from the truth about her husband's condition. She forbade the use of the word "cancer" before microphones. She rejected the release of several photographs because the tube in his mouth was too visible. She asked the

---

[23] Bill Kovach, "Rosalynn Carter still breaking barriers as a former first lady", *The Atlanta Journal And Constitution,* 12 July 1987, p. A11.
[24] Anthony, op. cit., p. 390.

doctors to stop talking to reporters because she had been disturbed by the amount of detailed information already made public about the president's health. In the weeks following the operation, she edited her husband's appointment calendar and managed her husband's staff to preserve a positive image of the president.

"I was told when I got there," a member of the White House press office said, "that if my name was in the paper commenting on Mrs. Reagan or her husband, the next time I would see my name in the paper would be the next day, that it would say that I was looking for work and that I would know that Mrs. Reagan had caused that to happen."[25]

Aides announced that she would have "veto power" over appointments. She also filled in for the president at official functions, with or without George Bush, the vice president.

On July 20, President Reagan addressed the nation in his weekly radio broadcast, thanking the hospital personnel and doctors. He then praised his wife and acknowledged her powerful role during the whole crisis.

"I'd like to indulge myself for a moment here. There's something I want to say, and I wanted to say it with Nancy at my side, as she is right now, as she always has been. First Ladies aren't elected and they don't receive a salary. They've mostly been private persons forced to live public lives. Abigail Adams helped invent America. Dolley Madison helped protect it. Eleanor Roosevelt was FDR's eyes and ears. Nancy Reagan is my everything." He then referred to her "strength", "support" and thanked her for "taking part in the business of this nation," concluding, on behalf of the American people: "thank you, partner, thanks for everything."[26]

But Nancy's protectiveness and power was not greeted by everyone with the same enthusiasm. It even offended some of her husband's associates who, as well as many journalists, regarded her as a sort of "associate president". She was called "the second most powerful person in the White House" in *Parade* magazine. One famous headline in *McCall's* read "Mrs. President", another in *The New Republic* "President Nancy."[27] She was compared to Edith Bolling Wilson who is said to have been "President-in-fact" for more than a year (from October 1919 to March 1921) while her husband Woodrow suffered a disabling stroke. She, too, had made sure the public did not know about the president's health. Hardly anyone saw Wilson on his sick bed and Edith cleared any document before it reached

[25] Joyce Gemperlein, « Nancy Reagan, protector, steps to the fore in a crisis », *The Philadelphia Inquirer*, 21 July 1985, p. A20.

[26] *My Turn*, op. cit., p. 279.

[27] *Parade*, 9 February 1986, p. 2; *McCall's*, November 1985, p. 117; *The New Republic*, 23 March 1987, p. 12.

him. She was even accused of signing her name to state papers. To some extent, this "Petticoat Government", as one furious opposition member of the Senate had called it at the time, also applied to Nancy's power.[28]

Nancy's manipulative "power behind-the-throne", denounced by many observers, proved especially true when, upon Ronald's return to the White House, she continued to press him to conclude the arms agreement with the Soviet Union. Columnist William Safire referred to it as the Nancyism syndrome: "the lust for an illusory quick-peace-fix to snatch a place in history."[29] Meanwhile, Ronald's popularity dwindled as his physical and mental capacities seemed to be declining, slowly but surely.

Nancy's deep concern for her husband and the power she used to defend him triggered off a very harsh confrontation with White House chief of staff Donald T. Regan. From the outset, Mrs. Reagan seemed to have disliked the man. Just like Lyn Nofziger a few years before, Regan's high profile and bossy style often pushed Nancy over the edge. Her impression was that he was unhelpful and self-seeking, working for his own interest, protecting his own image rather than that of the president, making decisions without consulting other staff members – or the First Lady – and overlapping on the president's turf. This she could not stand because it weakened Ronnie's image. When he was being treated for his colon cancer, she made her daily visit to the hospital by car while Don Regan used the presidential helicopter. The day she heard this, she was so outraged that Regan soon realized that he had better find a cheaper means of transport. He also talked too much to the press, she thought, explaining he had held the reins of the administration while the president had been in hospital. Really!

The First Lady-White House chief of staff relationship was characterized by a sort of permanent trial of strength, a cut-throat competition for power. And soon a major scandal would highlight this tension.

In November 1986, a month after a summit in Reykjavik, Iceland, where the Reagan-Gorbachev discussions had failed to produce agreement, disaster struck. Iran-Contra, the most serious crisis of the Reagan presidency, broke out. It was revealed that for fifteen months the White House had been involved in a secret deal with Iran. National Security Adviser Bud McFarlane and an NSC staffer, Lieutenant Oliver North, had been secretly selling arms to Iran in exchange for the release of American hostages held by Shiite Muslim terrorists in Lebanon. The profits from the sales were diverted to anti-Sandinista guerillas in Nicaragua, the "Contras". As Commander-in-chief, Ronald was held responsible for the crisis.

---

[28] Bernard A. Weisberger, « Petticoat Government », *American Heritage*, October 1993, p. 18.
[29] In Marci De Donald, « 'Mommy Dearest' », *MacLean's*, 16 March, 1987, p. 30.

He had violated his pledge never to deal with terrorist states and violated a congressional ban on aid to the Contras. In fact, this affair confirmed Reagan's detachment in the conduct of his administration and his excessive trust in the members of his staff, some of whom seem to have abused their power and hidden the truth from him.

Nancy, taken by surprise, would not let her husband's presidency be ruined by a case that he was not directly responsible for. "Every day Ronnie was being accused of things I knew he didn't do", she wrote in *My Turn*.[30] As the president went on the defensive, most headlines questioned his integrity. The whole nation was having doubts about its chief executive. The more he said he did not know about the diversion of funds, the less popular he seemed to become. According to a *New York Times*-CBS poll on December 1, 1986, his approval rating dropped from 67 percent to 46 percent in one month.[31]

Don Regan had carefully kept Mrs. Reagan "out of the loop" in this affair but, as Deaver later indicated, this was a gross mistake because she could have alerted her husband to its dangers. But the chief of staff would not have let a wife, even the president's, interfere in West Wing matters.

Nancy's strength was never greater than when it came to defending her Ronnie. She was determined to take charge and show the extent of her power. She vehemently blamed Regan for what had happened. "A good chief of staff has sources everywhere," she wrote in her autobiography. "He should practically be able to smell what's going on." Then she blamed him for keeping Ronald uninformed about what his staff had been doing in his name. She held Regan responsible for the president's poor performance at his first Iran-Contra press conference on November 19. Ronnie had been thrown into the media cage not knowing the true facts. Admiral John Pointdexter, who had replaced Bud McFarlane as National Security adviser, had provided him with incomplete information. She thought Regan should have made sure the briefing was accurate. Nancy was now a constant presence in the West Wing, visible or not. Regan complained he had to spend more time on the phone answering her questions than talking to the president.

What the chief of staff could not stand was her blind reliance on the occult. "Virtually every major move and decision made during my time as White House Chief of Staff," he wrote in his memoirs, "was cleared in advance with a woman in San Francisco who drew up horoscopes."[32] Nancy still took regular advice from Joan Quigley whose charts she used to determine the president's schedule, dates

[30] *My Turn*, op. cit., p. 319.
[31] *Ibid*, p. 320.
[32] In Anthony, op. cit., p. 383.

of speeches and conferences, domestic and international travel, even major political decisions according to the astrologer herself. She claims she was the one who recommended Reagan to give up his "evil empire" language before the Geneva summit. She also claims to have delayed the president's operation in July 1985 by three days.[33] Whether this were true or not, Nancy did not deny she regularly consulted Joan, "my friend", to protect Ronnie from unfavorable stars. Regan totally disapproved of this method of operating and was exasperated by the frequent changes of date for presidential meetings or the limitation on his public appearances that it necessitated. How could the chief of staff let the zodiac influence the political process?

The tug-of-war between Nancy and Regan escalated further in January 1987 when Ronnie returned to the White House after prostate surgery. The First Lady insisted on having him rest and recover for a while and refused to schedule a press conference on the Iran-Contra affair. Regan wanted the president to resume his regular activities to show people that he was in good health and was not unsettled by the scandal. She was focusing on the president while he emphasized the presidency. When Regan hung up on Nancy after she had called him and the two had had an extremely violent conversation, he had reached the point of no return. Nancy, who feared an impeachment procedure, had been more or less directly pushing her husband for Regan's replacement. As Ronald initially refused, she brought along old friends and allies such as Mike Deaver and Stu Spencer, together with Nixon's secretary of state William Rogers and Robert Strauss, a prominent Democrat, to persuade him. They eventually did and Nancy emerged victorious from the battle with the man who had once declared that women didn't understand anything about missile throw-weight.

On Friday morning, February 27, 1987, Regan was in the Oval Office discussing his retirement with the president. It was decided that he would leave the following Monday. In the afternoon, he was informed by Frank Carlucci, the new NSC chief, that CNN had released the news of his replacement as chief of staff by former Tennessee Senator Howard Baker. Elaine Crispen, Nancy's spokeswoman, had divulged the information to the press. In bitter disappointment, Regan left the White House right away. The press then reported Bakers's comments on the First Lady. He had confided to *Miami Herald* executive editor Heath Meriwether: "When she gets her hackles up, she can be a dragon." Later questioned on this declaration, he insisted that his remark was innocent. "The

---

[33] Henri Pierre, *La Vie Quotidienne à la Maison-Blanche au Temps de Reagan et de Bush.* (Paris : Hachette, 1990), p. 90.

First Lady is a distinguished citizen of this nation. She's a great lady and she obviously is a lady of strong convictions. That's what I meant."[34]

Some time after Regan was ousted, Nancy gloated in public before the American Camping Association that she was an expert in getting rid of leeches. Though she later denied referring to Regan, nobody missed the second meaning. On March 2, the date Regan had originally planned to move out of the White House, the media had a field day and condemned the First Lady with rare vehemence. Fred Barnes wrote in *The New Republic* that with Regan out, Nancy was now the new "chief honcho." William Safire, of the *New York Times*, was certainly the most virulent in his diatribe against Mrs. Reagan. In "The First Lady Stages a Coup", a vitriolic essay lampooning the First Lady's undue political power, he called Nancy "an incipient Edith Wilson, unelected and unaccountable, presuming to control the actions and appointments of the executive branch." He condemned her for making the president look ineffective and impotent: "At a time he most needs to appear strong, President Reagan is being weakened and made to appear wimpish and helpless by the political interference of his wife."[35] Cartoons popped up like mushrooms in which the First Lady was portrayed as the Dragon Lady, the castrating woman wearing the pants and "usurping" her husband's power. Some made fun of her overprotectiveness: Oliphant showed her brandishing a huge sword to defend her husband while he was innocently shuffling to bed in pajamas and dressing gown.

The president was understandably affected by the controversy over his wife's role in the Administration and he defended her as much as he could. He commented upon her so-called "power behind the throne" in an interview: "That is fiction," he said with some irritation, "and I think it is despicable fiction. And I think a lot of people ought to be ashamed of themselves."

The Tower commission, which had been appointed by Reagan to investigate the Iran-Contra affair, confirmed that the Administration had secretly traded arms for hostages and put the blame on Reagan's advisers, including Regan, rather than on the president in person. Yet it clearly criticized him for his absence of control.

It was on Nancy's advice that the president agreed to address the nation. He declared that the Iran-Contra affair should never have happened and he took responsibility for it. "It was a mistake," he admitted.[36] Though his declaration betrayed some detachment and a lack of conviction, this confession was politically necessary to regain some credibility after the firestorm. He was partly

---

[34] Owen Ullmann, « Remarks dog Baker on first day », *The Philadelphia Inquirer*, 3 March 1987, p. A12.
[35] William Safire, « The First Lady Stages a Coup », *The New York Times*, 2 March 1987, p. A19.
[36] Marion, op. cit., p. 270.

forgiven after his (semi-)confession and regained his confidence. But time had taken its toll on him and at seventy-eight he had lost his vigor and capacity to get over such emotional ordeals.

Trapped in the Iran-Contra imbroglio, unable to settle a dispute between his wife and his chief of staff, with a health crisis to crown it all, Reagan had lost his legendary drive. He looked despondent as he read the stream of poor comment in the press and saw public support drifting away from him. "Polls show Reagan Approval Rating at 4-Year Low" ran a *New York Times* headline.[37]

Like connected vessels, what one lost the other recovered. Though it was not premeditated, Nancy benefited from the situation. In the spring, after all the pungent criticisms in the press, a Gallup poll revealed that she enjoyed a 59 percent approval rating for the way she handled her role as First Lady. It also highlighted her impact on the administration as 62 percent of the American population believed that she had more influence on the president than any other First Lady before her.[38]

Nancy spent much of the rest of her husband's tenure explaining what her role was. In a speech to the American Newspaper Publishers' Association on May 4, 1987, she discussed the Reagan co-presidency. "I'm staffing the White House," she said, "and overseeing the arms talks. I'm writing speeches." Then she turned serious. "I'm a woman who loves her husband," she declared, "and I make no apologies for looking out for his personal and political welfare. We have a genuine, sharing marriage. I go to his aid. He comes to mine. . . . I have opinions; he has opinions. We don't always agree. But neither marriage nor politics denies a spouse the right to hold an opinion or the right to express it."[39]

The First Lady learned one great lesson from the flurry. She should now go back to exercise her influence inconspicuously, helping to make her husband look strong and decisive again. Otherwise, she might lose track of her primary goal: the success of Ronald Reagan, as a man and as a great president in American history.

In October 1987, it was Nancy's turn to look for support when she suffered her own health problems. Doctors diagnosed breast cancer. The crisis revealed the difficulty of her position as First Lady. Instead of opting for a lumpectomy, an option which would have been less radical for her figure, she decided to undergo a mastectomy, removing most of her left breast. "She realized she wouldn't be able to perform her duties," Ronald said, "if she had to undergo the radiation that

---

[37] Troy, op. cit., p. 304.
[38] « Poll Finds Most Back Role of Nancy Reagan », *The New York Times*, 10 May, 1987, p. A21.
[39] « Nancy Reagan Defends Her Right », op. cit.

would be required after a lumpectomy. . . ."[40] Nevertheless she had not anticipated the consequences of her decision.

The public debate that surrounded the surgery revealed the leading but delicate role of First Ladies. It was pointed out that Mrs. Reagan had set a bad example and might have prevented hundreds of women from seeking the right treatment. She was accused of running against the tide, annihilating years of effort from the medical world in terms of research and public information. In addition, the controversy about her hunger for power reappeared as some critics argued that to a certain extent, by cutting off her femininity, she had become more masculine.

Nancy was rather shocked by these accusations and she replied that whatever the option for treatment, cancer is a traumatic experience. She explained that her choice was a private, individual matter, not a model for others to follow. Yet it must be admitted that the woman, and of course the man, in the White House are not ordinary citizens and whether they desire it or not, they live in a fishbowl. The continuous exposure affords them little privacy. They are the center of attention, even when it comes to health care. This was as true for Nancy in 1987 as it had been for Ronnie in March 1981 or November 1985. Nevertheless, criticism of Nancy's decision was not unanimous. A number of people, even among her foes, praised the stoic grace she brought to this crisis. She was showered with get-well cards from around the country and received telegrams from prominent persons including Betty Ford and the Nixons. Even Raisa Gorbachev had flowers sent to the American First Lady. Also, the operation raised public awareness about breast cancer and it persuaded a lot of women to have mammograms. In this sense, the Nancy effect was quite positive.

Nine days after her operation, on October 26, Nancy suffered another loss: her mother Edith Luckett Davis, "Dee Dee", died at the age of ninety-nine. Having no time to rest, Nancy flew to Arizona to make the arrangements for the funeral. Then the Gorbachevs came to Washington and she had to fly back leaving her little time to grieve for her mother. 1987 had been a very trying year, she confessed, the lowest since 1981. Again she found comfort and relief in Ronnie who was as determined to support her as she had him. Love helped heal the scars.

The Reagan era in the White House ended on a double note of accomplishment, which Nancy had long pushed for. In June 1987, after a conference in Venice with the leaders of Japan, Canada, and Western Europe, President Reagan made a brief but significant visit to Berlin where, in front of the Brandenburg Gate, he issued a memorable speech, a challenge to the Soviet leader: "General Secretary Gorbachev," he said with striking emphasis, "if you

---

[40] Marion, op. cit., pp. 271-272.

seek peace, if you seek prosperity for the Soviet Union, if you seek liberalization: Come here to this gate! Mr. Gorbachev, open this gate! Mr. Gorbachev, tear down this wall!"[41] The much-publicized urge proved prophetic when on November 12, 1989, after years of antagonisms, the wall separating the two Germanys was knocked down, heralding the end of the Cold War. Symbolically, a 3,000-pound chunk of this wall stands today at the Reagan library in Simi Valley, California, to honor the fortieth American President.

At 2 p.m., on December 8, 1987, Mr. Reagan and Mr. Gorbachev signed the historic Intermediate-range Nuclear Force Treaty that sealed the common efforts of the two superpowers at ridding the world of the nuclear threat. The agreement also definitely established Nancy's husband as the man of peace she had so wanted him to be.

The 1980s ended with the departure of the Reagans from the White House in January 1989. After a very negative campaign which was declared "perhaps the most mean-spirited and negative campaign in modern-day American political history," Vice President George Bush had defeated Republican nominee Governor Michael Dukakis of Massachusetts in the November 1988 presidential election. His 53% to 46% victory marked the beginning of a new era in the nation's history and a new style in the White House. After eight years as Second Lady, Barbara Pierce Bush became the new hostess of the presidential mansion. Like Nancy, she had been a big asset to her husband's campaign. Unlike her, she had a naturally warm and down-to-earth attitude which made her look like "everybody's grandmother." She had four years to bring her own definition to the job of First Lady.

Though Ronald's two mandates represented just a short period in the Reagans' life, they had obviously been the most intense, depressing, exhaustive, exciting years they had ever lived. Lessons had been learnt and were still to be learnt from the experience. They both had had the same ambition: to make his presidency a triumph. That is why their partnership, in life and in politics, had operated so well. They had brought their own definition to the (co-)presidency. The two of them had benefited from their deep commitment to each other to overcome the strains of the job. "There's nothing more important," Ronald once said, borrowing his words from Clark Gable, "than approaching your own doorstep and knowing that someone on the other side of the door is listening for the sound of your footsteps."[42] Nancy always claimed that the key to his political success was their happy marriage: "The First Lady is, first of all, a wife. That's the

---

[41] http://www.conservativebeacon.com/ReaganResources.html
[42] In Chris Wallace, *First Lady: A Portrait of Nancy Reagan* (New York: St Martin's Press, 1986), pp. 24-25.

reason she's there. A president has advisers to counsel him on foreign affairs, on defense, on the economy and on politics. But none of those experts is there to look after him as an individual with human needs, as a flesh-and-blood person who must deal with the pressures of holding the most powerful position on earth."[43]

Yet it was this paradoxical combination of modernity and tradition embodied in their conspicuous love relationship that had raised the ire of the feminists who saw Nancy as an "anachronism": "She has not advanced the cause of women at all," had complained Feminist Author Betty Friedan, who graduated at Smith College, one year ahead of Nancy. "She is like Madame Chiang Kai-shek, doing it the old way, through the man."[44]

Their bond had also strained their relationships with their children. Michael had complained that his father had never seen his granddaughter Ashley until she was two years old. "I think they could live all by themselves and be perfectly happy", he once remarked, emphasizing their estrangement from their children. In 1986, Patti had written an autobiographical novel, *Home Front*, portraying a couple who sacrificed their children to satisfy their political ambition. Beth Canfield, the fictional Patti, complains that "the gap that separated us had become a chasm. . . ."[45]

It was hard to reconcile parents and children but leaving the White House eased the tension. As Ronnie and Nancy were released from the public duties, so they became more available to their family.

Greatly exhausted but proud to have served their country the best they could, the Reagans left Washington in January 1989. They were both looking forward to enjoying the pleasures of a peaceful retirement in California. . . .

---

[43] In "First Lady or second Fiddle", *Ladies Home Journal*, August 1987, p. 66.
[44] *Ibid.*, p. 86; *Time*, 14 January 1985, p. 10.
[45] Leighton, op. cit., p. 329.

Part VI

EPILOGUE: THE MOST FAMOUS CAREGIVER IN THE WORLD

The Reagans retired to a $2.5 million, 7,000-square-foot five-bedroom house at 666 St. Cloud Road in Bel-Air, California. Nancy had the number changed into 668 because of her superstitious belief that the triple six appealed to evil forces. Ronald moved into an office at 2121 Avenue of the Stars in Century City where he spent several hours a day assisted by a staff of twelve working on his own business as a former president. In order to keep in shape, he also worked out regularly and was often seen playing golf with friends or strolling on the beach with Secret Service agents. His mountaintop ranch, Rancho Del Cielo, was also a frequent retreat where he enjoyed chopping wood or riding horses.

After his forced resignation, Don Regan had written a book, *For The Record*, on his years in the White House and had excoriated the First Lady for her addiction to astrology and her orchestration of the president's staff's hirings and firings. In her turn, in collaboration with author William Novak[1], Nancy completed the writing of her memoirs, *My Turn*. In it, "for me, for our children, and for the historical record," she told her side of the story.[2]

In California, Nancy served on the board of directors of Revlon and pursued the great cause of her time as First Lady, the war on drugs. The Nancy Reagan Foundation of which she became the executive director, provided million dollar grants to drug prevention and education programs for America's youth, such as the Sherman Oaks-based BEST Foundation. As a survivor of breast cancer, she

---

[1] William Novak is well known for *Iacocca: An Autobiography*, a best-seller that he wrote with and about Chrysler's famous manager Lee Iacocca.

[2] Jacket copy of Nancy Reagan, *My Turn* (New York: Random House, 1989).

became a strong advocate of preventive health care for women. She brought her contribution by helping dedicate a Simi Valley prevention center that was renamed the Nancy Reagan Breast Cancer Center.

In November 1991, all five living American presidents and their wives, Richard and Patricia Nixon, Gerald and Betty Ford, Jimmy and Rosalynn Carter, Ronald and Nancy Reagan and George and Barbara Bush, together with another ex First Lady, Lady Bird Johnson, attended the official dedication of the $57 million Ronald Reagan Presidential Library and Museum in Simi Valley, thirty miles north of Los Angeles. This ceremony was a historic one as it marked the largest gathering ever of American Presidents and First Ladies. It was also one of the last great events in the life of the Great Communicator that he was fully aware of. In the summer of 1993, during his annual checkup at the Mayo Clinic in Rochester, Minnesota, he was diagnosed as having the degenerative Alzheimer's disease. One year later, on November 5, 1994, he decided to make it public in a poignant letter to the nation. "I now begin the journey that will lead me into the sunset of my life. I know that for America there will always be a bright dawn ahead. Thank you my friends. May God always bless you."[3]

Shortly after this public announcement, the Reagans were contacted by a research and support group from Chicago, the Alzheimer's Association. Some time later, this research initiative bore a new name: the Ronald and Nancy Reagan Research Institute.

The emotional burden of the disease fell heavily on the former First Lady but she was not about to collapse. In one of her last political battles, she pilloried retired Lt. Colonel Oliver North when he was running for a U. S. Senate seat for Virginia in 1994. North had published a book, *Under Fire: An American History*, in which he accused Ronald Reagan of giving his go-ahead to the Iran-Contra arms deal. The former marine had written that he was "convinced President Reagan knew everything." One month before the election, Nancy told a reporter that the man "lied to my husband and lied about my husband."[4] Her statement was widely reported in the media and prevented North from winning office. When it came to protecting Ronnie's reputation, she was strong enough to force his enemies to retreat. Though she was no longer the "Dragon Lady", she could still spit some fire. When years before at MGM, she had been asked what her rule of life was, she had answered that she believed in the law of retribution: "You get what you give."[5] It seemed that she still stuck by the same rule.

---

[3] Ronald Rreagan's letter to the nation, November 5, 1994. Property of the Ronald Reagan Library, Simi Vallley, California.
[4] Helen Thomas, "Nancy's a trouper until the very end", *Daily News*, 23 July 2001, p. 7.
[5] Cf. *Supra*, p. 27.

Then, Alzheimer took its toll and Ronnie's health kept deteriorating. Many faces faded from his memory, including his own children and, presumably, his own wife. He was no longer capable of having a sensible conversation.. His privacy was understandably guarded by his family and he was not seen in public any more. Nancy kept vigil over her husband and took on the role of companion, protector and nurse. She became his main caregiver, "the most famous caregiver in the world" as she was called in cancer circles. The disease had brought sadness in their relationship but their love seemed more real than ever. "To watch them is very romantic" said John Hutton, Ronald's physician and long-time friend.[6]

Once criticized for being too protective of her husband, Nancy was now praised for the same reason. Here was one more paradox in her life. She was perceived in a new light and her resilience was unanimously acknowledged as she continued to appear at various meetings in her own name or representing her husband at official events. One of those took place in a moving and memorable appearance at the Republican National Convention in San Diego on August 12, 1996. Her eyes glistening with tears, the tiny little lady addressed the delegates and spoke publicly about her husband's life, alleviating the pain of his absence by reading an extract of his last political speech four years before at the party convention of 1992. A tearful crowd greeted her performance with a rousing round of applause and a standing ovation.

In late 1996, Nancy put Rancho Del Cielo, Ronnie's cherished ranch in the Santa Ynez mountains, up for sale for $6 million. The old man was no longer able to go there and ride his favorite black thoroughbred, Little Man, across the hills above Santa Barbara. The estate was sold in April of 1998 to Young America's Foundation. Since then, the Ranch in the Sky, the Ranch of Heaven as Ronald used to call it, has been preserved in its authentic condition and has been used as an educational facility to honor the memory of the former president.

Not the least of paradoxes in the whole Reagan experience was the family reunification that Ronnie's illness succeeded in accomplishing. Soon, everyone was getting along fine but the sad thing was this recovered harmony came too late for Ronnie to recognize. Patti, who had often rebelled against her parents, took comfort in being closer to them now. Pondering over her relationship with her dad and mom since her birth, she wrote in July 2002: "The circle always brings us back around. And when it does, we have a chance to offer the best of ourselves to the ones who waited for us to grow into who we were always meant to be."[7] Patti was also convinced that her father sensed that she and her mother patched up their

---

[6] William Plummer, et. al., « Endless Love », *People*, 13 March 2000, p. 133.
[7] Patti Davis, « We remain connected to the ones we love", *Parade Magazine*, July 28, 2002, p. 17.

differences and reconciled. "(Patti) thinks he has gotten a feeling of the two of us together and, as she says, his soul doesn't have Alzheimer's," Nancy said to CBS's Mike Wallace on "60 Minutes II" (25 September 2002).

Like Nancy, Maureen, Ronald's child from his first marriage, had devoted much of her time to raising awareness of Alzheimer's disease since her father was diagnosed as suffering from the debilitating disorder. She joined the Alzheimer's Association national board in 1999 and in October 2000, she received the Alzheimer's Association Distinguished Service Award. Yet her crusade against her father's disease did not save her from her own fatal illness. Melanoma, an incurable skin cancer struck the sixty-year-old author of *First Father, First Daughter: A Memoir* (1989). She died in her home at Granite Bay, California, near Sacramento on August 8, 2001.

Nancy now seldom leaves her Bel-Air mansion and no visitors are allowed in. Her rare public appearances are mainly reserved for the Reagan Library on which occasions she devotes a few hours to signing her autobiography. Her latest stand is now the research on embryonic stem cells. She strongly believes that it could uncover a cure for Alzheimer's. In 2001, she wrote a letter to President George W. Bush in which she expressed her wish to see federal support for the research. The Republican Party was divided on the issue and because researchers must destroy human embryos to get the cells, a practice known as "therapeutic cloning" that pro-life groups strongly opposed, the president restricted federal funding. Nancy believed a lot of time had been wasted and a lot of people had suffered and died because of the current lack of action. In her letter, she let the president know that "my husband and I believe our legacy should be that no other family should have to go through what our family has been through."

Most observers recognize that Ronnie was always Nancy's vital force. Even though Alzheimer curtailed her enthusiasm and made her life sad and lonely, her dedication to his well-being never failed and her love always remained intact. "I can't remember life before Ronnie," she said umpteen times. "Everything began with him, and he's been my whole life."[8] Though it sounds like a cliché, the statement is hard to counter. Nancy cherishes the time when Ronald would send flowers to her mother and thank her for having given him Nancy, when he would leave love notes and letters to his "dear "Mommie Poo Pants" ending "I.T.W.W.W.," an acronym from "I love you more than anything . . . . in the whole wild world."

Throughout Ronald's gradual decline, Nancy will have brought her husband what little comfort he may have been able to enjoy though it is doubtful he has

---

[8] In Jeff Wilson, « Nancy :'I can't remember life before Ronnie », *Daily News*, March 3, 2000.

ever realized her constant presence was guided by love. But she has always had the firm conviction that through her tender affection, he could still see "the shining city on the hill, a place full of hope and promise."[9]

[9] Nancy used the metaphor in her 1996 address to the Republican Convention. She had borrowed it from Ronald himself who had quoted John Winthrop who on the deck of his *Arabella*, had told a group of pilgrims that "we shall be as a city upon a hill." In Peter Hannaford, *The Reagans: A Political Portrait* (New York: Coward-McCann, Inc., 1983) p. 136.

NANCY REAGAN'S FILMOGRAPHY

The Dr. and the Girl
1949
With Glenn Ford, Charles Coburn and Janet Leigh

East Side/West Side
1950
With Ava Gardner, Cyd Charisse, James Mason and Barbara Stanwyck

Shadow on the Wall
1950
With Zachary Scott and Ann Southern

The Next Voice You Hear
1950
With James Whitmore

Night into Morning
1951
With Ray Millard, John Hodiak and Jean Hagen

It's a Big Country
1952
With Gary Cooper, Gene Kelly, George Murphy and Janet Leigh

Shadow in the Sky
1952
With James Whitmore and Jean Hagen

Talk About a Stranger
1952
With George Murphy

Donovan's Brain
1953
With Lew Ayres

Rescue at Sea
1955
With Gary Merrill

Hellcats of the Navy
1957
With Ronald Reagan

BIBLIOGRAPHY

ADLER, Bill. *Ronnie and Nancy: A Very Special Love Story*. New York: Crown Publishers, 1985.

ANDERSON, Alice E. and Hadley V. Baxendale. *Behind Every President: The hidden power and influence of America's First Ladies*. New York: SPI Books/Shaposky, 1992.

ANDERSON, Martin. *Revolution*. New York: Harcourt Brace Jovanovitch, 1988.

ANTHONY, Carl Sferrazza. *First Ladies: The Saga of the Presidents' Wives and their Power, 1789-1990*. 2 vols. New York: Morrow, 1990, 1991.

----------. *America's First Families*. New York: Touchstone, 2001.

BARRETT, Laurence I. *Gambling with History: Reagan in the White House*. New York: Penguin Books, 1983.

BIRMINGHAM, Stephen. *California Rich*. New York: Simon & Schuster, 1980.

BLUMENTHAL, Sidney, and Thomas Byrne Edsall, editors. *The Reagan Legacy*. New York: Pantheon Books, 1988.

BOLLER, Paul F. *Presidential Wives*. New York: Oxford University Press, 1988.

BOYARSKY, Bill. *Ronald Reagan: His Life and Rise to the Presidency*. New York: Random House, 1981.

CANNON, Lou. *Reagan*. New York: G. P. Putnam's Sons, 1982.

----------. *President Reagan. The Role of a Lifetime*. New York: Simon & Schuster, 1991.

CARDIGAN, J. H. *Ronald Reagan: A Remarkable Life*. Kansas City: Andrews and McMeel, 1995.

CAROLI, Betty Boyd. *America's First Ladies*. Pleasantville, New York: Reader's Digest, 1996.

----------. *First Ladies: An intimate look at how 36 women handled what may be the most demanding, unpaid, unelected job in America.* New York: Oxford University Press, 1987.

DAVIS, Loyal, M. D. *A Surgeon's Odyssey.* New York: Doubleday & Co., 1973.

----------. *Go in Peace.* New York: G. P. Putnam's Sons, 1954.

----------. *J. B. Murphy: Stormy Petrel of Surgery.* New York: G. P. Putnam's Sons, 1938.

DAVIS, Patti. *Deadfall.* New York: Crown Publishers, 1989.

----------. *Home Front,* with Maureen Strange Foster. New York: Crown Publishers, 1986.

DEAVER, Michael K. with Mickey Herskowitz. *Behind the Scenes: In which the author talks about Ronald and Nancy Reagan...and himself.* New York: Morrow, 1987.

----------, with Nancy Reagan. *A different Drummer:* My Thirty Years With Ronald Reagan. New York:, 2001.

ELWOOD, Roger. *Nancy Reagan: A Special Kind of Love.* New York: Pocket Books, 1976.

EVANS, Rowland, with Robert Novak. *The Reagan Revolution.* New York: E. P. Dutton, 1980.

FEINBERG, Barbara Silberdick. *America's First Ladies: Changing Expectations.* New York: Franklin Watts, 1998.

GOULD, Lewis L., ed. *American First Ladies: Their Lives and their Legacy.* New York: Garland Publishers, 1996.

GUTIN, Myra G. *The President's Partner: The First Lady in the Twentieth Century.* New York: Greenwood Press, 1989.

HANNAFORD, Peter. *The Reagans: A Political Portrait.* New York: Coward-McCann, 1983.

HERTSGAARD, Mark. *On Bended Knee: The Press and the Reagan Presidency.* New York: Farrar, Straus & Giroux, 1988.

KELLEY, Kitty. *Nancy Reagan: The Unauthorized Biography.* New York: Pocket Star Books, 1991.

LEAMER, Laurence. *Make-Believe: The Story of Nancy & Ronald Reagan.* New York: Harper and Row, 1983.

LEIGHTON, Francis Spatz. *The Search for the Real Nancy Reagan.* New York: Macmillan, 1987.

MARION, Kati. *Hidden Power: Presidential Marriages that Shaped Our Recent History.* New York: Pantheon Books, 2001.

MAYO, Edith P; and Denise D. Meringolo. *First Ladies: Political Image and Public Portrait.* Washington D. C.: Smithsonian Institution, 1994.

MELANDRI, Pierre. *Reagan: Une Biographie Totale*. Paris: Laffont, 1988.

MORRIS, Edmund. *Dutch : A Memoir of Ronald Reagan*. New York: Random House, 1999.

NOONAN, Peggy. *When Character Was King*. New York: Viking Penguin, 2001.

PEMBERTON, William E. *Exit With Honor: The Life and Presidency of Ronald Reagan*. Armonk, N.Y.: M.E. Sharpe, 1997.

PIERRE, Henri. *La Vie Quotidienne à la Maison Blanche au Temps de Reagan et Bush*. Paris : Hachette, 1990.

QUIGLEY, Joan. *"What does Joan Say?"*. New York: Birch Lane Press, 1990.

REAGAN, Maureen. *First Father, First Daughter: A Memoir*. Boston: Little, Brown & Co., 1989.

REAGAN, Michael, with Joe Hyams. *On the Outside Looking In*. New York: Zebra Books, 1988.

REAGAN, Nancy with Bill Libby, *Nancy*. New York: Berkeley Books, 1981.

----------, with William Novak. *My Turn*. New York: Random House, 1989.

REAGAN, Ronald. *An American Life: An Autobiography*. New York: Simon and Schuster, 1990.

----------. *Speaking My Mind*. New York: Simon and Schuster, 1989.

----------, with Richard C. Hubler. *Where's the Rest of Me?* New York: Duell, Sloan & Pearce, 1965.

REGAN, Donald T. *For the Record: From Wall Street to Washington*. New York: Harcourt Brace Jovanovitch, 1988.

ROSEBUSH, James. *First Lady, Public Wife: A behind-the-scenes history of the evolving role of First Ladies in American political life*. Lanham, MD: Madison Books, 1987.

SMITH, Elizabeth Simpson. *Five First Ladies*. New York: Walker & Co., 1986.

STOCKMAN, David. *The Triumph of Politics: Why the Reagan Revolution Failed*. New York: Harper & Row, 1986.

THOMAS, Tony. *The Films of Ronald Reagan*. Secaucus, N. J.: Citadel Press, 1980.

TROY, Gil. *Affairs of State: The Rise and Rejection of the Presidential Couple Since World War II*. New York: The Free Press, 1997.

TRUMAN, Margaret. *First Ladies: An Intimate Group Portrait of White House Wives*. New York: Random House, 1995.

WALLACE, Chris. *First Lady: A Portrait of Nancy Reagan*. New York: St. Martin's Press, 1986.

WATSON, Robert P., ed. *American First Ladies*. Pasadena, Ca.: Salem Press, 2002.

WHEELER, Jill. *Nancy Reagan*. Leading Lady Series. Edina, Minn.: Abdo & Daughters, 1991.

WILLS, Gary. *Reagan's America: Innocents at Home*. New York: Doubleday & Co., 1987.

INDEX